A Light Upon My Path

Daily Devotions for Advent & Christmas

#2694

ISBN: 978-0-88028-526-1

Forward Movement
inspire disciples. empower evangelists.

A Light Upon My Path

Daily Devotions for Advent & Christmas

Contributors

Phil Beyer, Jazzy Bostock, Laurie Brock,
Lester Mackenzie, John Ohmer, and Joseph Yoo

FORWARD MOVEMENT
Cincinnati, Ohio

Editor's Note

In the middle of the ocean, the stars are magnificent. No longer obscured by light pollution, they delight the night, sparkling, a few flitting here and there.

I imagine the shepherds enjoyed the same celestial dance. Without artificial light, they could see the glory of creation on a nightly basis. What an amazing backdrop for the angel of the Lord, who brings "good news of great joy." The light of the stars guides the shepherds on their path to see the child "born this day in the city of David a Savior, who is the Messiah" (Luke 2:10-11).

In the Gospel of Matthew, we hear of another star playing a, well, starring role. Sent on a journey to "search diligently for the child," the Wise Men follow the star of Bethlehem to the house where the child was "with Mary his mother; and they knelt down and paid him homage" (Matthew 2:11). How brilliantly that star must have shone to stand out among all the others in the night sky to serve as a beacon—a guiding light—for the Wise Men.

During the seasons of Advent and Christmas, we hear a great deal about light. Indeed, we await and then celebrate the arrival of the Light of the World. My hope is that these meditations, offered faithfully by talented writers—clergy and lay—will be a companion on your journey. I pray that as you seek and serve the Light, these reflections may be like the tapestry of stars guiding the shepherds, a beacon for the wise men and women still seeking the child today.

This book can be used each year as you make your way toward the manger. The meditations are drawn from Year One or Two of the Daily Office readings or Years A, B, or C of the Revised Common Lectionary readings for the seasons. In addition, depending upon when Christmas lands, I invite you to skip ahead to that meditation and then follow along through the twelve days of Christmas (and, if you have time, go back and read the reflections you skipped!).

Sometime during this journey, I also hope you will take time to go outside, away from city lights. In a field, perhaps, or atop a mountain. Spend time with the stars and with all of creation, giving thanks for their light upon your path.

Richelle Thompson
Editor

A Light Upon My Path

I
Advent

Sunday

Be on guard so that your hearts are not weighed down with dissipation and drunkenness and the worries of this life, and that day catch you unexpectedly, like a trap. For it will come upon all who live on the face of the whole earth. Be alert at all times, praying that you may have the strength to escape all these things that will take place, and to stand before the Son of Man.

—Luke 21:34-36

Jesus isn't trying to scare us with these words from the Gospel of Luke. He's urging us to wake up.

Advent is a season of anticipation. But we're not talking about the anticipation of what presents may be waiting for us underneath the Christmas tree.

Advent is about the arrival of Jesus, the Light of the World stepping into the darkest of places. This reading calls us to pay attention, to open our eyes, and to see where Christ's light is already breaking through.

Jesus says in Luke 21:28, "Now when these things begin to take place, stand up and raise your heads, because your redemption is drawing near."

This is a reminder that no matter how heavy, chaotic, or dark life feels, God's plan continues to unfold. The same God who promised a Savior to Israel keeps promises today. That promise? Redemption is near.

Maybe the signs Jesus describes aren't so different from what we experience now. Headlines scream news of wars, disasters, and division. It's easy to feel like the world is falling apart. But Advent flips our perspective. Instead of looking at the chaos and despair, we're invited to look for hope—to seek out the flickers of Christ's light, sometimes faint but always present.

Jesus urges us to stay awake, not in fear but in hope. Hope that the worst things will never be the last thing. Hope that the light will grow brighter, revealing God's kingdom here on earth.

So, how do we stay awake? We stay awake by noticing where God is at work in our lives and the world. We show kindness when it's easier to remain indifferent. We pray, even when words feel hard to find. And we trust that God's redemption is as real today as it was when Jesus was born.

In the season of Advent, we're called to wait. But this is not a passive waiting. It's active, expectant, and grounded in faith. Think of a fig tree, as Jesus mentions earlier in Luke. When the tree sprouts leaves, you know summer is near. The signs of God's kingdom are just as real—if we pay attention. A kind word to a stranger. A reconciliation long overdue. A small act of generosity. These are the leaves sprouting in our world, pointing us to the hope of Christ's light.

This Advent, let us stay awake. Let us stay hopeful. And let us remember: the story doesn't end in darkness. Jesus is the Light who came into our world, and his light still shines. Stand tall. Raise your head. Redemption is near.

—Joseph Yoo

PRAY

JESUS, LIGHT OF THE WORLD, help me to stay awake this Advent season. Open my eyes to the signs of your love and your kingdom breaking through. When fear and doubt creep in, remind me of your promise: redemption is near. May I carry your light into the world, bringing hope to those who need it most. *Amen.*

Monday

They are like trees planted by streams
of water, bearing fruit in due season,
with leaves that do not wither;
everything they do shall prosper.

—Psalm 1:3

I think of this metaphor often. Not the one about the righteous prospering and the wicked losing because that, frankly, doesn't feel very honest to what I see and know from the world. Rather, I often think about being planted by streams of water. Jesus frequently refers to himself as living water in the gospels, a crucial source of nourishment and refreshment. Water is so basic to life: to growth, to hygiene, to survival. We cannot live without water.

Similarly, we cannot live without Jesus. He is crucial to our systems and to our lives. The Word of God sustains and nourishes us, cleansing and refreshing our souls.

So, how do we plant ourselves near that living stream? How do we ensure our roots are deep and drinking from the flow Jesus provides?

One of the ways we are nourished in the Spirit is through scripture. Now, don't get me wrong: I don't wake up every morning and spend time reading the Bible. I wish I did, but that pattern doesn't work in my chaotic life. Instead, I get in my scripture time through sermon preparation. I sit deeply with the readings assigned, letting them nourish my roots. Perhaps your practice is reading these devotions or taking home the Sunday worship bulletin to study. Your spiritual practice doesn't have to be hard—but it does need to be practiced!

Another way we plant our roots in the living stream is through prayer. Again, I don't have a stringent prayer practice; my way of prayer is more conversational. I chitchat with God, remarking on the beauty of a cloud, giving thanks for crossing off a task from my to-do list, or asking for help to focus. Prayer can look a thousand different ways, but I think we know when we are praying because of how we feel. For me, I come away from prayer with an inner peace.

The last way I think we are nourished by God's flowing stream of living water is through time spent together. Sometimes this is in scripture, and sometimes in prayer. But I also believe an essential element of my relationship with Christ is nourished by being with God—just sitting and recognizing God's presence in and around me. I don't need to talk or read or do anything—just pause for a moment and feel.

—Jazzy Bostock

PRAY

GOOD AND GRACIOUS GOD, with this next breath I take, nourish me. Let me feel your water flowing over my heart, refreshing and renewing. Help me to stay rooted here, in this place with you, that whatever may come my way, and whatever this day may hold, I would be able to feel your strength in this place and hold on to your peace. *Amen.*

Tuesday

Therefore the wicked shall not stand
upright when judgment comes,
nor the sinner in the council of the
righteous. For the LORD knows
the way of the righteous,
but the way of the wicked is doomed.

—PSALM 1:5-6

✠

As we enter into this holy season of preparation to celebrate the coming of Jesus, I invite you to join me in examining these words from Psalm 1: "For the LORD knows the way of the righteous, but the way of the wicked is doomed." Without mincing words, this passage calls us to evaluate how we can act to further unity, not separation, and nurture much-needed transformation and hope.

In this psalm, we are called to a life firmly planted in the love and goodness of God. This call has nothing to do with a checklist of rights and wrongs or judging how valuable we are based on how much good we've done. It's about living in the kingdom where we are dependent on one another, dependent on God, and dependent on the gift of creation.

We are interconnected. As a South African Californian shaped by a Sub-Saharan African theology, I am reminded of this interconnectedness. In 2002, I spent nearly 8,000 miles in a van, crossing the United States and visiting places of deep pain and violence for an initiative called Hands in Healing. These experiences led me to embrace the African Ubuntu wisdom, "I am because you are." I cannot heal without you. Without each other, we cannot recover from wounds of division, injustice, and neglect.

Psalm 1 paints a beautiful picture of this truth in the tree planted by streams of water. This tree doesn't fight or force; it stands and is fed from its source and, over time, grows and produces fruit. Righteousness is hinged upon God's love, not out of work and effort but as an answer to grace.

Advent calls us to live out that love by nurturing creation and seeking justice. This is not an easy task. Seeking racial justice, caring for our earth, and working for equity can seem overwhelming and impossible. But Psalm 1 reassures us that we are not alone. As a tree cannot live without water, we cannot live without the infinite love and light of God.

The early Christian desert mothers and fathers knew something about this. Still and strong, they were. Rooting themselves in God's love, they reminded us to take time to quietly draw closer to God's presence so we might be renewed for the journey.

This Advent, may we, guided by God's love and light, recognize we are one people, one family, and one force of love and light. Armed with the insight, wisdom, and traditions of the people of the Way, we stand together in Christ's calling for justice, care of the earth, and nurturing relationships that mirror God's reign where everyone has a seat at the table.

May we stand like trees by rivers of living water bearing fruit in due season, not a casualty of life's storms. Let us flee from the passing away of evil things, which are like grass that withers in the sun. When we travel this way, God walks beside us and carries us with love, directing our way with light and urging us to spread that light into a tired world.

May this Advent time fill us with the love and light of God.

—Lester Mackenzie

PRAY

O GOD OF MERCY AND JUSTICE, you watch over those who walk in your way. May you fill our hearts with the peace of knowing you are in our midst, walking beside us every step of the way. Give us the strength to make this journey. Root us deeply in your love in this season of waiting. Help us to care for the earth in which you have placed us. Give us strength to stand boldly against this broken world and to rise with courage to seek integrity. Let us keep our hearts set on the hope of the coming of Christ. Make us steadfast when the road is hard. Remind us of your peace when we are weary. Tear down the walls of oppression and build communities of righteousness and grace. *Amen.*

Wednesday

When the scribes and chief priests
realized that he had told this parable
against them, they wanted to lay hands
on him at that very hour,
but they feared the people.
So they watched him.

—LUKE 20:19-20A

Advent is the first season of the church year, beginning four Sundays before Christmas. Advent, from a Latin root that means "arrival" or "waiting," developed in some ways as a mini-Lent, a preparation time before the Feast of the Nativity. In the ancient church, Advent may have encompassed the six Sundays before Christmas, which would mess up the symmetry of Advent candles and wreaths in our modern church. We eventually settled on four. Traditions of Advent have included fasting and penance, as in Lent. But Advent is not Lent. They might be sister seasons, but they are distinct, as well. While Lent is a season of penance, Advent is a season of waiting.

And that probably explains why we make Advent a season it is not. Instead of dropping into the deep wretchedness at worst and annoyance at best of waiting, we divert ourselves from this particular quality of Advent by leaning very much into Christmas.

And I completely understand why.

Waiting is not fun.

Spend a day at the local department of motor vehicles. Go on the last day of the month, when all the people who didn't renew their tags or licenses are there. Go there and stand. And wait. And stand. And wait. And wait.

Go on.

I'll wait.

Or go to an event where the speaker is fifteen, twenty, thirty minutes late. How quickly do we start to complain and make observations about the leader not being courteous during our time? How quickly do we become annoyed that we have to wait?

See, waiting isn't fun. It's annoying, troubling, and hard. It's difficult to find the holiness in waiting. We are, by and large, an impatient people. From our ancestors in the faith to the current church, we want God to act now and with haste on our timetable.

And God just laughs.

Because waiting is anything but speedy. Waiting is that moment after you've pruned the tree. It looks bare and ragged. Gashes show where old branches used to grow, the ones that had become too heavy or were dying or needed to be pruned to encourage new growth. Waiting is the space between the actual pruning and the spring blooms, where the tree seems to be doing nothing but looking scraggly. Waiting is the moment between Good Friday and the Resurrection, when the tomb is sealed and filled with the dead body of Christ. Waiting is the silence after Jesus says, "Then give to the emperor the things that are emperor's, and to God the things that are God's." We know the people who asked him the question were waiting for him to pick door number one (pay taxes, which would mean support the Roman Empire) or door number two (don't pay taxes, which would break the law). So, there they were, waiting to respond with their answer. Not all waiting is holy.

But some is—and Advent calls us into that holy waiting where we settle, however uncomfortably, into the slow work of God.

Advent is best understood as a season pregnant with hope for what is to come. Mary figures quite prominently in Advent, as she should. It is a season of the holy feminine, carrying something new within us, within our community, that which is waiting to be born yet needs time to gestate.

This wisdom, in part, is that a life of faith involves cycles of waiting, when the old has been removed but the new has not yet been born. God needs holy things to gestate within our souls and our communities. These holy ideas, understandings, insights, and actions all need time to become. If they are born too early, at our demanding impatience, they cannot survive. God knows the exact time of birth. We usually do not.

And so we must wait. We must wait for the growth to begin, to mature. We must wait through the discomfort, even the sickness, as we allow the new thing to develop. We must wait for the labor pangs. We must wait for the water and blood to rush forth, heralding the birth. We must wait.

Advent draws us into this truth of life, of the immense importance of waiting. For four Sundays, we hear the cries of a people, of our own souls, wanting to know when, how, and why. For four Sundays, we encounter Mary, a young woman heavy with the holy Child gestating within her, waiting. For Advent, we stand in lines, pace the halls, feel uncomfortable, and sit in tears at our frustration with the act of waiting for something, anything, to be born.

We do not like waiting. And yet, God knows that we must wait as God waits.

The poet Rilke writes, "You must give birth to your images. They are the future waiting to be born. Fear not.... The future must enter you long before it happens. Just wait for the birth, for the hour of new clarity."

Advent matters because it is the holy season of waiting for the birth. The birth of Jesus, the birth of new ideas, the birth of courage, the birth of new songs and dreams, and the birth of what God has impregnated within us that is gestating.

—Laurie Brock

PRAY

GOD OF SLOW WORK AND SILENT WAITING, give us grace and courage to see the holiness in the events that unfold gradually, the dreams that unhurriedly gestate before they can be born, and the wisdom whose meaning comes in minute revelations rather than immediate insight. May we, with Mary, wait for your love to be born into our lives; through your Son, Jesus Christ, we pray. *Amen.*

Thursday

How can we thank God enough for you in return for all the joy that we feel before our God because of you?

1 Thessalonians 3:9

Erin reached the bottom of her Christmas stocking. Finding nothing, she turned it upside down and shook it. She glared at me, "Where is my Christmas letter?" I shrugged, "Well, I'm getting old and …" She cut me off, wagging her finger, "No way!" "Your Christmas letter is always my favorite gift!" I looked at her older brother, Chris, and my wife, Jeanie, for support but found none. Chris said, "You can't play the old-age card, Dad. We all look forward to your letters." Jeanie smirked, nodding in agreement. A lesson learned: some traditions should endure, particularly the expression of love.

For more than 30 years, I had written each family member a Christmas letter, a love letter, and slipped it into their Christmas stockings amongst the oranges, walnuts, and candy canes. Written words sometimes had to serve for the words I could not utter in person of how proud I was, not so much for their accomplishments but for who they were and becoming. I wanted them to know that as they sailed the rough seas of life, I remained their safe harbor in which they could always anchor. There were always things to write about because life happens: graduations, heartaches, new jobs, Jeanie's ordination and ministry, marriages, extended family, deaths, babies, and family gatherings.

The next Christmas, their letters were snuggly in place. To my surprise, I found a scroll in my stocking tied with red ribbon. Jeanie, Erin, and Chris had written me a combined love letter. Gulp. I tried reading each word, but my tears wouldn't permit it. I wanted to steal away to a quiet place and sob.

The apostle Paul was a prolific writer whose letters uttered words of encouragement to fledgling churches when he could not be present. Paul wrote letters from his heart, impassioned and intensely personal. Churches were like his offspring. In Thessalonians, Paul beseeched church members to remain faithful and sent Timothy to encourage them and not to be shaken by persecution. Upon Timothy's return, Paul wrote, "How can we thank God enough for you in return for all the joy that we feel before our God because of you?"

Love letters have an impact. They reach into the heart and often into the eye's plumbing. I've found that letters need not be eloquent. What is heartfelt is the intention… someone loved enough to write.

—Phil Beyer

PRAYER

O Lord, we praise your holy name, for in the beginning was the word, and the word was made flesh that shines forth in our hearts and all the earth. Inspire the words of our hearts to proclaim the new light, Jesus, our Savior, the fulfillment of all who have gone before. *Amen.*

Friday

Once more Jesus spoke to them
in parables, saying:
"The kingdom of heaven may be
compared to a king who gave a wedding
banquet for his son."

MATTHEW 22:1-2

✠

When Jesus talked about the kingdom of heaven, he used parables and extended metaphors to paint vivid mental pictures for us. In this passage, Jesus compared the kingdom of heaven to a banquet (we might say a lavish dinner party) hosted by a king for his son's wedding.

The early church would have connected the dots in this parable. They would have known that the guests who refused invitations to join the king's banquet were the same people Jesus referred to as wicked tenants in a previous parable, the religious leaders who crossed the road in the parable of the good Samaritan, or the petulant older son in the parable of the prodigal son.

These folks, Matthew's readers would have known, are anyone (or any one of us!) who, out of busyness, greed, misguided theology, jealousy, or any other reason, refuse to join the feast that God invites us to.

Jesus wanted to make it clear that it's not only those we consider "good people" who are invited into the kingdom of heaven but also those whom we consider "bad people." And because the church—the Body of Christ alive in the world today—is one of the ways God's heavenly will is "done on earth as it is in heaven," that means that both good and bad are parts and essential members of the church. That includes not just the early Christian church but the church today: your church and mine and all those around the world.

Moreover, it is not only the good and bad people who are part of the kingdom but also the good and bad of you and within you that are welcome. Your light and your dark, the brightness of your personality, and the shadow side of your personality are proactively and profoundly invited to and included at the table, the banquet of God's grace, and then sent forth to further God's mission.

Remember this. Remember that "church" is a place, a people, and a movement where you are invited and already inside not because you deserve to be but because God chooses to invite and bring in both good and bad—all good and bad people and all the good and bad of you.

And then also remember this: precisely because you have received grace, be graceful. That's why Jesus's parable ends with the story of the person thrown out of the banquet because he was not appropriately dressed. When we are at the banquet of grace, we should clothe ourselves accordingly. It's not about changing our outfits; it's about changing our outlook.

We are invited and included in God's kingdom work. So, we should wear the garments we've been given: divine compassion, kindness, and patient forgiveness. If more of us did that, more of God's kingdom would come, and more of God's will would be done on earth as it is in heaven.

—*John Ohmer*

PRAY

Loving God, by your grace, I have been invited to and included in your heavenly banquet, the kingdom of God on earth. By your grace, I have received your compassion, kindness, and patient forgiveness. Help me today to clothe myself with the divine outfit you have given me: the outlook of compassion, kindness, and patient forgiveness. *Amen.*

Saturday

Jesus, aware of their malice, said,
"Why are you putting me to the test,
you hypocrites?"

Matthew 22:18

Jesus always seems to have the perfect response, which is something I envy because most of my perfect responses come to me in the shower way after the interaction.

The religious leaders try to trap him with a question about taxes, but Jesus flips their trap into a more profound teaching about identity and allegiance. At first glance, this story doesn't seem to have anything to do with Advent. But it does. Quite a bit, actually.

In Advent, as we prepare our hearts to make room for Jesus, we're also invited to reflect on what it means to follow Jesus, to belong to him. Just as the coin bore Caesar's image, we bear the image of God. Genesis 1:27 reminds us that we are created in God's image, stamped with divine approval and worth. And that means our ultimate allegiance isn't to anything in this world but to God.

But the world tries to claim us in other ways. It wants us to define ourselves by our achievements, possessions, and status. We are being pulled in so many directions, and it becomes easy to lose sight of whose image we bear. We get caught up in the busyness of life, especially during this season. There are parties to attend, gifts to buy, Christmas cards to send, and decorations to hang. These aren't bad things. However, the busyness of the holidays can pull us away from the deeper meaning of Advent if we are not mindful.

When Jesus talks about giving to God what is God's, he is inviting us to give God our whole selves—not just an hour on Sunday mornings or a quick blessing before meals. Jesus is inviting us to give our lives, our hearts, our love, all that we are, all that we have to God because all of it belongs to God because we belong to God.

I challenge you to ask yourself this question during the Advent season: Am I living as someone who bears the image of God? Is my life reflecting the light of Christ?

Jesus is reminding us that the world doesn't define who you are. Your accomplishments and accolades, the talents you bring to the table, aren't the things that define you. Your identity, your purpose, and your worth come from God.

On one of the windows of our storefront church hangs a banner that says:

No matter what
the world
the politicians
your diagnosis
social media
your income
say about you,

you are a beloved child of God.

With all that I am, I believe that about you.

Advent isn't just about looking forward to Christmas—it's about remembering who we are and whose we are and living in a way that reflects that truth.

So, whose image do you bear? When people look at your life, do they see the light of Christ shining through? This Advent, let us live as those who belong to God, letting God's love guide our actions and God's light shine through our lives.

—Joseph Yoo

PRAY

LORD, I belong to you. Help me to live as someone who bears your image, reflecting your light and love in all I do. This Advent, let my heart be fully yours, and may my life point others to the hope and joy of Jesus, the Light of the World. *Amen.*

II
Advent

Sunday

A shoot shall come out
from the stump of Jesse,
and a branch shall
grow out of his roots.

Isaiah 11:1

As we journey through this season of Advent afresh, I find myself drawn to this question: how does Isaiah's ancient vision speak to us today?

In the Church of the Province of Southern Africa and apartheid South Africa, I grew up to learn that waiting is not a passive act but a vibrantly, dynamically alive and active process. Waiting is often a type of wrestling with the very present that we are in while withholding thc hope of a coming and promised future. It's most obvious when you take on the injustices around you. Isaiah isn't just speaking poetry here; he is inviting us to imagine, to savor a new world that God is bringing into being.

Isaiah gives us the stirring image of a shoot growing from the stump of Jesse, the ancient name for the emblem of the family that inhabited Bethlehem, the birthplace of David. This image sustains me in moments when hope seems far away, and justice seems improbable. Today, I invite us to consider Isaiah's call: What does that "shoot" mean in terms of our ministries? How can we feed the poor, offer shelter to the meek, and produce places of peace, trustworthiness, and reconciliation in our communities?

Isaiah has given us a fearless challenge that can transform us. But this vision is more than a prophecy of the Messiah's coming. It is a call to action to all who lead and serve to embody divine wisdom and justice. In the minds of ancient Israelites, their king was an embodiment of God's justice and wisdom, a man who would rule just as God would. How can we bear that same spirit of wisdom and justice today?

This is not simply passively waiting for something to happen; it is passionate anticipation. This scripture invites us to look for what is not yet clear and gives us eyes to see the shoots of hope already appearing in surprising places. True peace—*shalom*—is not the absence of conflict, says Isaiah. It's all about justice, restored relationships, and communal flourishing.

Until Christ comes again, we are to labor in our communities and see them become homes where wolves and lambs, lions and calves can abide together in peace.

This Advent, I offer you three words to carry in your hearts: root, equity, and *shalom*.

Root acts as a reminder of God's enduring promises and the stories through which our faith shapes us.

Equity requires us to act justly and to take responsibility.

Shalom is dynamic and transformative, convoking us into just relationships within and beyond.

Let us accept the invitation of Isaiah's vision. May we have faith in the shoot that issues from the stump of Jesse. Let us dare to be that shoot for others. Amen.

—Lester Mackenzie

PRAYER FOR COMMUNITY

O GOD OF NEW BEGINNINGS, you bring life from what feels lost and call me to hope in your peaceful kingdom. I confess, Lord, that I fear socially constructed differences and cling to comfort instead of love. But you call me to build a community where all belong, held in justice and care.

Give me courage to face my fears, to hear hard truths, and to walk with others on the path of healing and peace. Root me in your love, guide me with wisdom and strength, and help me live as a witness to your hope in the name of the one who unites us. *Amen.*

Monday

The same day some Sadducees came to him saying there is no resurrection, and they asked him a question: "Teacher, Moses said, 'If a man dies childless, his brother shall marry the widow and raise up children for his brother.' Now there were seven brothers among us; the first married, and died childless, leaving the widow to his brother. The second did the same, so also the third, down to the seventh. Last of all, the woman herself died. In the resurrection, then, whose wife of the seven will she be? For all of them had married her."

MATTHEW 22:23-28

At one level, this exchange between Jesus and the Sadducees is about resurrection—certainly a deep and important theological issue! But it can also be read at an even deeper level: as a commentary on the ways we question God.

Take a close look at the question in the passage above. The Sadducees's question, "In the resurrection, then, whose wife of the seven will she be?" comes only after a complicated, bizarre, and tragic hypothetical situation that they've made up based on a Levitical law that required a man's brother to marry the widow if his brother died leaving his wife childless.

What if, they ask, a woman has to marry all seven brothers of her late husband, one right after the other, because none of the marriages to those brothers produced a child? When the woman dies, and there is a resurrection, which husband has her as his wife?

"Jesus answered them, 'You are wrong, because you know neither the scriptures nor the power of God. For in the resurrection they neither marry nor are given in marriage, but are like angels in heaven'" (Matthew 22:29-30).

Jesus is responding to the Sadducees, but he's not really answering the question they asked. As is so often the case when Jesus runs up against legalists—people who care more about religion than God—Jesus will not be trapped. Rather, he is saying, in effect, "I'm rejecting the premise of your question."

This passage can challenge the way we question God. Often, when we ask questions of God, rather than answer, God responds by saying, essentially, "Your question is based on a worldview that I seek to subvert. You might be quite confident in that worldview. It may give you a sense of comfort and predictability. But it also happens to be wrong."

That is one of the things I love about the Bible. As Madeleine L'Engle says about scripture in her book, *The Irrational Season*:

> As a young woman, I turned to the Bible for purely literary reasons. But I discovered that the Bible is a great deal more alive than the Church establishment seemed to be. It is a repository of joy and piety and history and humor and storytelling and great characters, and my writer's mind was nourished. I stayed with the Book all through the years when I kept my back turned on the Establishment.

The Bible, as the word of God, is a great deal more alive than any establishment, and this passage, in particular, invites us to think about the questions we ask God.

If we're not getting a direct answer, might we ask ourselves if our question is based on an unimaginative or stale assumption or a worldly premise that God seeks to subvert?

—John Ohmer

PRAY

O God, by whom the meek are guided in judgment, and light rises up in darkness for the godly: Grant us, in all our doubts and uncertainties, the grace to ask what you would have us do, that the Spirit of wisdom may save us from all false choices, and that in your light we may see light, and in your straight path may not stumble; through Jesus Christ our Lord. *Amen.*

—The Book of Common Prayer

Tuesday

Give thanks in all circumstances; for this is the will of God in Christ Jesus for you. Do not quench the Spirit.

1 Thessalonians 5:18-19

My wife, Jeanie, dropped a bomb as the family sat around the dinner table: "How about this Christmas, we go to Haiti on a medical mission?" Our teens, Christopher and Erin, let their forks drop to their plates. I choked on my burger: "We talked about a Caribbean trip…but Haiti?"

Two months later, we arrived in Haiti, fully vaccinated, our suitcases bulging with donated giveaway clothes and medications. Conditions in Haiti were oppressive—extreme poverty, filth, polluted water, and protesters burning tires. We drove in the darkness along the potholed road toward our base camp. For miles, burning candles lined our path by candleholders hopeful that we would pause to buy their life-sustaining wares.

That Christmas, my family and the medical mission team built relationships with Haitians in remote villages instead of building sandcastles on a beach. Erin held and sang to infants as she dropped vitamin A in their eyes and multivitamins on their tongues. Chris became the impromptu pharmacist providing medicines to patients who had just visited the doctors. Alongside Haitian priests and seminarians, Jeanie and I served on prayer teams, anointing hundreds with oil.

My soul searched for answers. How can people whose lives have been devastated by hurricanes, earthquakes, violence, and famine still give thanks? How many times can one be flattened, face to the earth, and still pull oneself up to one's knees to praise God? Given most Haitians' circumstances, I wondered if I possessed the faith to arise singing each morning, as many Haitians did.

My questions were answered by those who sought prayer. I was on holy ground in prayer circles, listening to their sacred stories. I was invited in. I couldn't be so cavalier as to embody their life circumstances but only be so humble as to taste a morsel of their painful but hopeful humanity. Most came to pray with dancing eyes and contagious smiles. Their prayers were of gratitude for babes in arms, healing, their crops, and safety. Their hope was in God and their community of resolute believers.

I mistakenly believed I was transporting hope to Haitians in overstuffed suitcases. Hope already resided in the congregations we visited. They make do. They pray, mourn, dance, and rejoice together.

I savored worshiping with Haitian congregations, swaying to the beat of a conga drum and hearing the Episcopal liturgy sung in French and Haitian Creole, different languages from mine but the same rhythm of one God, one faith, and one shared burning hope of the resurrection.

—*Phil Beyer*

PRAY

DEAR LORD, in times of trial and tribulation, grant us the courage to face our challenges with unwavering strength. Help us to rise above adversity, trusting in your divine plan. May we find resilience in our struggles and hope in our hearts. *Amen.*

—Mason Caldwell, Haitian prayer

Wednesday

Woe is me! I am lost, for I am a man
of unclean lips, and I live among a people
of unclean lips; yet my eyes have seen
the King, the LORD of hosts!

ISAIAH 6:5

Most of us know the beautiful hymn, "Here I am, Lord," written based on the words Isaiah speaks a few lines later in Isaiah 6:8. These words from verse 5 don't make such compelling hymnody. Still, I would venture a guess that most of us have felt exactly what Isaiah is expressing here.

I see Isaiah's words as an expression of self-doubt. Isaiah sees God—the hem of God's robe filling the temple with an awe-inspiring grandeur—and Isaiah's response to it all is one of self-doubt. Woe is me! I am not worthy!

I suspect many of us have responded to God in a similar way. Far too often, our response when God calls us is self-doubt. We might hear that voice calling in the night, beckoning us to take on a new mission or ministry, but then we think, "No, not me. There must be someone better suited to all of this."

The response to Isaiah's self-doubt is rather severe. One seraphim flies over to Isaiah with a burning coal and touches it to his lips, metaphorically (and literally) burning his self-doubt away. Following the excision of self-doubt, Isaiah is free to speak his famous words, "Here am I; send me!"

We often get in our own way when it comes to fulfilling the calls God puts on our lives. We doubt our skills, our worthiness, our capacity. I am reminded of something author Marianne Williamson once wrote that it is our light, not our darkness, that most frightens us. Heeding God's call and responding with, "Here I am, send me," doesn't leave room for self-doubt. We need to be ready to show up with all of the light that is inside of us, with all the skills and capacity God has already given us to fulfill what we are being asked.

I have a lot to learn from Isaiah. My self-doubt often gets in the way, and sometimes I fall into the trap of making space for it, of coddling my ego by believing that I am too weak or too young or too female, or too...fill in the blank. Isaiah reminds me that this self-doubt doesn't come from God and must be removed, even by burning coal, so I am ready to respond, "Here am I; send me!"

—Jazzy Bostock

PRAY

ALMIGHTY GOD, you are so big that even the hem of your robe would fill our cathedrals. In the face of such grandiosity, I can feel so small. Remind me, especially in those moments, that you have called me for such a time as this. Burn out the doubt that threatens my willingness to respond to you and make me ready to accept whatever steps you may place before me. *Amen.*

Thursday

I saw the LORD standing beside the altar, and he said: Strike the capitals until the thresholds shake, and shatter them on the heads of all the people.

AMOS 9:1A

✠

Amos delivers this message to me in such a way that snaps me awake from my state of unconsciousness. I cannot ignore this call. I face God in complete exposure because there remains no way for me to conceal myself. God is issuing me a call through this experience.

I had long misunderstood the concept of judgment found in Amos. The vision in this passage appeared horrifying because I believed it had been sent to destroy everything.

Through the wisdom of the ancestors, I understand better what is happening. According to Ubuntu teachings, our lives connect to the whole community, which means God's assessment leads us to seek proper relationships with others.

I cannot run from the truth. God's judgment seeks to transform my existence rather than destroy it. Through its purifying function, I experience accountability that transforms me into a spiritually maturing person.

The Light of the World Jesus exposes me to healing instead of shame. Jesus's light illuminates those spaces I try to avoid, when I select greed and hoarding instead of fairness, and when I stand idly in passive silence amid injustice.

Yet true love requires me to accept responsibility. Following Jesus means I must pick truth instead of self-protection and practice humility rather than exercise pride. The wider church must do the same. Our healing process starts with judgment rather than ends with it. God's justice is real. Righteousness still matters. The arrival of light begins a permanent transformation in everything.

—Lester Mackenzie

PRAY

GRANT, O GOD, that your holy and life-giving Spirit may so move every human heart [and especially the hearts of the people of this land], that barriers which divide us may crumble, suspicions disappear, and hatreds cease; that our divisions being healed, we may live in justice and peace; through Jesus Christ our Lord. *Amen.*

—The Book of Common Prayer

Friday

When the hour came,
he took his place at the table,
and the apostles with him.

—Luke 22:14

Meals are an important part of this season. Before the endless holiday movies, Santa Claus, Christmas trees, and Advent wreaths, we celebrated this season with meals.

The Twelve Days of Christmas in Tudor, England, called for twelve days of feasting. Roasted meats, puddings, pies, and stews filled tables. Work ceased. Mulled wine and ales flowed. Games, celebrations, singing, and dancing filled the days after the faithful gathered for prayers on each holy day of Christmas.

Preparing for this massive feast took a while. Tudor cooks did not run down to the local farmers' market or grocery stores to pick up ingredients for the meals. Meats had to be hunted and prepared; smoking, salting, and curing took time. Puddings and pies were labor and time-intensive. Ales and wines were not brewed overnight. Most of the citizens were not wealthy, so to have enough for the feasts, a time of fasting helped stock the larders.

The meals that were such an integral part of the Christmas celebration took time, focus, and attention as they were prepared. Flour, yeast, water, and honey were blended to create the basic recipe for bread for the table. Human labor kneaded and pushed and pulled the dough as the disparate elements married each other. Then the dough rested, a step as important as kneading for a good bread. Only with this work and rest did they have the bread to be made holy for the feast.

And wine? Pressed grapes, water, and time meld together. Aging and fermentation create the wine that, for centuries, has been a staple to all tables.

But even before that, farmers tended the soil, planted seeds, and nurtured stalks of wheat and vines of grapes. The fruits of the harvest were gathered at the appointed time, then ground and stomped and dried and aged so they could be transformed into meals.

Advent was (and still is for some) a time of fasting and preparation. Christians in past eras took the days of Advent with a true sense of preparing for the feast. They ate less to have more for the Christmas feast. They spent time preparing food to laden tables. They prepared for the feast of Christmas by engaging in the work of Advent.

I wonder if, with our modern conveniences around preparing meals, we've lost a bit of the ancient wisdom of Advent. Perhaps our fasting in Advent calls us to focus on the many ways we humans are intertwined through our meals. What if we fasted from not noticing and instead were attentive to our meals, the food we ate, and the stories they might tell us about how God's creation nourishes us? What if we allowed our meals to invite us into prayer—for the soil and water and sun and seasons that create the foundation for our food to grow; for the farmers and workers who plant seeds and grow livestock and fish; for the workers who harvest and prepare our food; for the drivers who transport it to our farmers' markets and grocery stores; for the employees who stock shelves and keep stores clean; and for the recipes we use that may be from a website or handed down from ancestors?

When Jesus invites his disciples to share in the Lord's Supper, he invites us into a meal that asks us to be attentive, aware, and mindful. We as Christians must pay attention to the plight of the world around us, how we can heal the broken world, and the small aspects that too many don't notice. We do not get the option to ignore how connected we all are. Instead, we must see the feasts of our lives, whether the Holy Eucharist, Christmas dinner, or the lunch we eat each day, as holy invitations to prayer and awareness.

—*Laurie Brock*

PRAY

BLESSED ARE YOU, LORD OUR GOD, King of the universe, who creates varieties of nourishment. This Advent, may we be mindful of the many who work for the food we eat. We give thanks for all who have been part of the community who worked to bring this meal for our nourishment, especially those we name either silently or aloud. Nourish our bodies with this food, our souls with the connections to those who grew and prepared it in any way, and our lives with the faith that fills us. *Amen.*

Saturday

As Jesus came out of the temple and was going away, his disciples came to point out to him the buildings of the temple. Then he asked them, "You see all these, do you not? Truly I tell you, not one stone will be left here upon another; all will be thrown down."

Matthew 24:1-2

The disciples must have been stunned when Jesus predicted the destruction of the temple. The temple was the center of their faith, a symbol of God's presence among them. But Jesus points them beyond brick and mortar to something far greater: a kingdom that will never crumble.

Jesus speaks of wars, famines, earthquakes, and persecution, but while unsettling, this message isn't one of despair. Jesus is calling us to endure. To trust. To keep our eyes fixed on the unshakeable hope of God's kingdom.

Advent is a season of waiting and preparations, but it is not a passive season. It's about standing firm in faith even when the world around us feels unstable. Jesus's words remind us that the things we often rely on—our achievements, our plans, even our places of worship—are temporary.

At the time of writing this, the headlines of today make Jesus's warnings feel way too real. Hearing the news and knowing the work ahead can leave us feeling weary.

But Jesus reminds us to not be alarmed. These things are not the end but the beginning of something new. The brokenness around us is still part of God's redemptive plan.

So, we move forward with our eyes fixed on Jesus and only Jesus, resisting being swayed or led astray by false prophets who claim to have easy answers or quick fixes. In Advent, we are reminded to stay rooted in the truth of not only who Jesus is but also to whom we belong.

That's the invitation of Advent: to hold on to hope, trust in God's faithfulness, and live as citizens of God's eternal kingdom.

So, how do we endure? By staying connected to Jesus, the Light of the World. By nurturing our faith through prayer, scripture, and community. By looking for glimpses of God's kingdom breaking through—in acts of kindness, moments of forgiveness, and the quiet assurance that God is with us.

Advent reminds us that we're part of a story bigger than the chaos of today. The temple may fall. The earth may shake. But the love of Christ and the promise of God's kingdom will never fail.

—Joseph Yoo

PRAY

LORD JESUS, amid uncertainty and change, help us trust in your unshakable kingdom. As we wait for the celebration of your birth and the fulfillment of your promises, teach us to endure with hope and faith. Let your light shine through us, bringing peace to a weary world. *Amen.*

III
Advent

Sunday

When John heard in prison
what the Messiah was doing, he sent
word by his disciples and said to him,
"Are you the one who is to come,
or are we to wait for another?"

Matthew 11:2-3

Many churches are full or nearly full on Christmas Eve. Even churches that only get a handful of people on a typical Sunday tend to have larger numbers of worshipers on Christmas Eve.

Have you ever paused to wonder why? Why do people come to church on Christmas Eve?

I think people come to church on Christmas Eve for some of the same reasons people do on Sundays or other occasions. Obligation is one of the reasons; others are habit or tradition.

But I think a significant motivation for many people is that they—we—are stressed. When I say stressed, I don't necessarily mean that in a negative sense. I mean that we are stressed in the way a rope is stressed when it is in use. That stress—that tension—can be good. It means the rope isn't just lying around, slack, but being used for the purposes for which it was created. Folks come to church, I think, because they feel tension, something pulling at them. Saint Augustine said, "You have created us for yourself, dear Lord, and our hearts are restless until they rest in you." To put it another way, inside of us is a God-shaped hole that only God can fill.

That's why people come to Christmas Eve services. They long for the mystery of God incarnate…made real, practical, and tangible.

Granted, we may not articulate that: we may not say, while grabbing our keys on the way out the door, "Hey hon, bye, I'm on my way to be confronted and comforted by the transcendent mystery of God and to have my life transformed through the Holy Spirit to more fully and joyfully live out my calling to be the unique part of the Body of Christ I was created to be. Back in about an hour."

But that's what Christmas Eve services and all liturgies are meant to do.

If a church service does its job—and by "church service," I mean the whole experience: the worship part of the service, including the readings, prayers, music, preaching, and sacraments, and equally important, a sense of authentic hospitality and community, all driven by a unifying, outward-facing vision—then people will be brought face to face with God.

And these encounters with God lead to transformed lives. We leave church feeling more fulfilled because our God-shaped hole is being fully filled. We sense that our stress, our tension, is serving its purpose.

—John Ohmer

PRAY

O God of unchangeable power and eternal light: Look favorably on your whole Church, that wonderful and sacred mystery; by the effectual working of your providence, carry out in tranquility the plan of salvation; let the whole world see and know that things which were cast down are being raised up, and things which had grown old are being made new, and that all things are being brought to their perfection by him through whom all things were made, your Son Jesus Christ our Lord; who lives and reigns with you, in the unity of the Holy Spirit, one God, for ever and ever. *Amen.*

—The Book of Common Prayer

Monday

They will look to the earth,
but will see only distress and darkness,
the gloom of anguish; and they will be
thrust into thick darkness.

Isaiah 8:22

The light of their childhood innocence was darkened by homelessness, gangs, drugs, and now prison. They were mistrustful of me, their teacher, the do-gooder white dude three times their age. As fifteen hardened faces stared at me from around the table in the prison chapel, I agonized, "How do I reach them?"

"Coloring books" was God's answer to me in my desperate prayers while driving home. "Wait, What?" But I decided to listen and try it, so at the next class, I piled the gift of brand-new coloring books and crayon boxes on the table. "There are enough for everyone, they're yours." I took mine and began coloring.

Shortly, all of the inmates except Taylor thumbed through their coloring books and started coloring. Taylor sat back, arms across his chest, glaring, until he asked, "What are you doing here, old man?" I dropped my crayon, speechless. All eyes were on me, waiting. I finally said, "I've asked myself that. Honestly, I'm winging it, following God's lead." Taylor refolded his arms and grunted, "Huh," still refusing to color.

What followed was surreal. Men who had walked in darkness trafficking drugs, violence, and people were now coloring, laughing, kidding one another, holding up their coloring book creations…just as children do in their innocence. And, as children often do when coloring, they told stories.

Simpson unwrapped the paper from a crayon. "At school, I stole crayons and ate them on the way home 'cause I had no food." Gibson's tornadic circles in his coloring book personified his chaotic childhood: "Never even went to school, lived wherever, sold oxy." Mills held up his coloring book: "This is my first gift ever. I never had birthdays or a

Christmas." "Prison saved my life," Hawkins said. "All the brothers I ran with are dead."

Coloring books and crayons were the outward and visible light of God's grace: unexpected, freely given, enough for all…no nubs, scraps of paper, or hand-me-downs. God's light overcame the darkness and distrust brooding in the chapel, giving way to laughter and glimmers of childhood innocence.

The inmates wanted to color again next time. On his way out, Taylor grabbed the remaining coloring book and crayons, "See ya next week."

—*Phil Beyer*

PRAY

Be near me, Lord Jesus, I ask thee to stay, Close by me forever and love me I pray. Bless all the dear children in Thy tender care, And take us to heaven to live with Thee there.

—"Away in a Manger"

Tuesday

The people who walked in darkness
have seen a great light;
those who lived in a
land of deep darkness—
on them light has shined.

Isaiah 9:2

✠

I know this darkness. I was born into it. Apartheid South Africa applied substantial pressure that twisted my thinking. Unfair laws transformed victims and beneficiaries into people who accepted their inferior or superior status. When I first arrived in the United States, I thought I would be able to sever my connection to darkness. However, it remained concealed within redlines along with reservations and prisons, which represented fresh names for historical deceptions.

Darkness serves to oppress and trap all those who come near it. Archbishop Desmond Tutu explained through his teachings that treating others as less human causes us to become less human as well. Injustice poisons the soul. A person who maintains power over another remains bound by the constraints of oppression. Both apartheid and racism produce captives instead of victims on every side of their operation.

I stood at Red Shirt Table in South Dakota, where the land continues to mourn the tragedy of the Wounded Knee massacre. The wind transported grief and the profound loss of ancestral traditions. At that moment, I fully understood how slavery makes everyone captive. The injustice belongs to no one specifically—those who lost their land nor those who gained it from the theft. All people experience captivity from the force of marginalization and the centering power of dominance. All members of society stay trapped within the deceitful system of white supremacy that functions as a foundation for domination.

Isaiah exposes this darkness in his prophecy, yet he never stays focused on this aspect. Through his vision, Isaiah guides our eyes to observe the Light that is breaking through: the child born to us, a son from God who carries the titles Wonderful Counselor, Mighty God, Everlasting Father, Prince of Peace.

The Light does not emerge to create peace for people who remain content with their situation. It comes to set us free. The Light eliminates the false connections between being superior and inferior to others. This Light prevents us from being comfortable in systems that cause both oppression and destruction of those being oppressed and those who oppress. The Light advances in this relentless journey without any possibility of stopping.

The period of darkness needs to end. Freedom demands something of us. It requires truth. It requires justice. We should examine our hands to observe our personal pain—and the damage we have inflicted on others. Jesus, who serves as Light of the World, shows a healing touch and an ability to expose. We find healing when we embrace the Light, which transforms us in our march toward the Beloved Community.

The Light has dawned. We need the strength to approach and live this vision afresh.

—Lester Mackenzie

PRAY

A Prayer for Intsapho yabantu –
the Human Family
(Xhosa tradition)

O God of Truth and Justice,
Unveil the truth that divides us.
Shred the fears that keep us silent.
Break the chains—of power, privilege, and pride—
that blind us to the sacred worth of every human being.
Give us the audacity to speak,
the strength to stand,
and a love so fierce that no barrier can withstand it.
Until no one is master,
no one is slave,
and all your people walk free in your Light. *Amen.*

Wednesday

As it is written in the prophet Isaiah,
"See, I am sending my messenger
ahead of you, who will prepare your
way; the voice of one crying out in
the wilderness: 'Prepare the way of the
Lord, make his paths straight.'"

MARK 1:2-3

The Third Sunday of Advent is often called Stirrup Sunday, a name taken from the first words of the collect for this week. As a horse person, I find special meaning in this name.

When humans and horses began partnering, humans rode bareback and grabbed a handful of the horse's mane to hold on. While that may have been a good beginning, this particular style of riding was not helpful in the long term for the rider or the horse. While most horses are rideable at the walk, when they start to move faster, say at a trot or gallop, we need some help to stay on. Without stirrups, that help is not present.

I have to think early riders spent lots of time on the ground.

Eventually, humans, being the inventive bunch we are, created a saddle. The earliest saddles appeared about 800 BCE and were probably no more than thick fabric pads. After a time, riders determined that a tree, a piece of wood that formed the spine of the saddle, worked even better to support a rider on a horse.

But the game changer for riders and horses? The stirrup.

We don't know exactly when or where the stirrup was added to the saddle. Most equine historians estimate the stirrup was developed in Asia some 1,000 years after the saddle made its appearance. The stirrup did some amazing things for horses and riders. The stirrup works with the saddle to help the rider balance. With feet in stirrups, a rider can better control the horse with leg pressure. Stirrups are important for balance and control so the rider can more securely ride a horse at higher speeds. With the stirrups, riders are less likely to fall off their horses.

These rather unimpressive parts made of leather and metal or wood are, quite honestly, some of the most important elements in the rider-horse partnership. They provide balance, direction, and assistance to us to create a beautiful relationship between horses and humans that benefits both.

We pray this week for God to stir up God's power to come among us to help and deliver us because we humans are a messy lot. We fail to love as Jesus loved us. We hold grudges that damage relationships. We don't live out our promises made at Baptism. We get lazy with our prayer life and our worship. There's a list of ways we become unbalanced and directionless in our life of faith.

Like the first riders who climbed on the back of a horse, we are okay at a slow speed. Our faith may be quite fine as long as life is neat and tidy, going as we expect.

But life rarely stays at that speed. Life will speed up. Too many things happen at once, and we feel overwhelmed. We are overwhelmed, stressed, and anxious. When life speeds up, we get dislodged, we fall, we stumble, and we are sitting on the ground, bruised and sore, not sure what to do.

Advent is a season to recognize that God provides spiritual stirrups for us, which help prepare the way so we might find balance. Like stirrups, God's life aids are rarely impressive. God comes among us in Advent in small and ordinary ways to provide us with balance, direction, and assistance. These small ways can look like a few moments of quiet when we light our Advent candles at home, read the Holy Scripture or listen to Advent music, write a letter to a friend, or take a walk and simply notice God's creation as we walk.

Life can be fast and unyielding at times. That is simply life. And God comes among us, often in quiet ways, to give us peace, holiness, and balance, stirring up the elegant quiet that is the calm in the tempests of life.

—Laurie Brock

PRAY

STIR UP YOUR POWER, O LORD, and with great might come among us; and, because we are sorely hindered by our sins, let your bountiful grace and mercy speedily help and deliver us; through Jesus Christ our Lord, to whom, with you and the Holy Spirit, be honor and glory, now and for ever. *Amen.*

—The Book of Common Prayer

Thursday

The loving-kindness of the LORD
fills the whole earth.

PSALM 33:5B

It's a beautiful sentiment, isn't it? The earth is full—brimming to the top—with God's steadfast love. And yet, sometimes, that's far from our experience. If I am lucky, I experience the fullness of God's love maybe once or twice a week. Often, on Sunday mornings, something happens in worship with others that reminds me that God is all around, all the time. And sometimes, during the week, if I really challenge myself to see it, I might pause enough to feel or see God within and around me. But, all too often, I miss it.

Advent is a time of waiting: not just waiting for Christmas, Santa, or carols to blare out of every shop window, but waiting for Jesus. It is waiting on a few different planes. We wait for Jesus to be born in the stable in Bethlehem. We wait for Jesus to come again, one day, to set things right here on earth, and we wait for Jesus to be born anew in our hearts and lives. That last one is where I often fall short—and where I need to focus my attention.

The story of Jesus's birth is not just a one-time miracle but a promise that God is with us, then and now and into the future. And the inspiration of Christmas isn't just that Mary said yes, but that in her yes, she encourages us to similarly embrace God's presence in our lives and our very flesh. This advent of Christ, then, is not just happening in us but surely, as the psalm says, through the whole earth. The earth is full of the steadfast loving-kindness of the Lord because Jesus is born again and again in each moment we breathe.

Looking around for signs of that steadfast love might be a gratitude practice or, as I sometimes think of it, a delight practice. Look for something that delights you each day. Notice how God is making Godself known to you. I believe that the earth is full of the steadfast love of the Lord because we are full of that love.

—Jazzy Bostock

PRAY

O God, the whole earth is full of your love: the trees, the flowers, the grass, the very soil itself. Give me eyes today to see that love in others and in myself and to have the courage to bring you to birth in me and my life. *Amen.*

Friday

Are you the one who is to come,
or are we to wait for another?

Matthew 11:3

It's a strange question, especially if you think about who is posing the question.

It's John the Baptist, the cousin of Jesus, the one who in his mother's womb leapt at the sound of Mary's voice, the one who preached that he was not worthy to carry the sandals of Jesus, the one who baptized Jesus.

This is the person who's asking Jesus if he is the one.

What happened to John that he is no longer certain about Jesus's identity?

Well, for starters, John is asking this question while stuck in prison, uncertain of what may come next. And Jesus never came to visit and (worse, perhaps?), Jesus hasn't done anything to get John out.

Jesus isn't showing up in the way that John expected Jesus to show up.

Haven't we all had moments when God didn't meet our expectations or show up in the way that we desired God to show up? Maybe we prayed for healing, and it didn't come. Maybe we expected smooth sailing after committing to follow Jesus, but life got harder.

John's question feels raw and honest (sometimes more than we allow ourselves and other Christians to be): "Jesus, are you who I thought you were?"

And in typical Jesus fashion, he doesn't respond with a simple yes or no. Instead, he points to what's happening: the blind see, the lame walk, lepers are cleansed, the deaf hear, the dead are raised, and the poor have good news brought to them. In other words, "John, I'm doing exactly what the Messiah was promised to do. You just weren't expecting it to look like this."

Advent is a season of expectations. We decorate, light candles, and prepare for Christmas with specific ideas in mind. But what if Jesus shows up in ways we didn't expect? What if he's more interested in healing the broken and bringing hope to the hopeless than fulfilling our carefully laid-out plans?

Jesus goes on to praise John, calling him the greatest born of women. But then he flips it again: even the least in the kingdom of heaven is greater than John. Why? In God's kingdom, greatness isn't about your résumé or how loudly you preach repentance. It's about trust and our willingness to love beyond ourselves; it's about being part of the new thing God is doing.

Here's the Advent challenge: Are you expecting a cozy season with pretty lights and familiar carols? Or are you open to seeing Jesus in unexpected places—in the face of a stranger, in a moment of forgiveness, in the quiet nudge to step out of your comfort zone?

Jesus didn't meet John's expectations, but he exceeded them. The same is true for us. Advent isn't about a Messiah who fits neatly into our plans; it's about a Savior who shatters our expectations and invites us into something better: a kingdom where light overcomes darkness, and love transforms the world.

—Joseph Yoo

PRAY

JESUS, help us let go of our expectations and open our hearts to how you move in the world. When we feel disappointed or confused, remind us that your plans are always greater than ours. May your light shine through us this Advent season, even in the unexpected. *Amen.*

Saturday

John said to the crowds that came
out to be baptized by him,
"You brood of vipers! Who warned you
to flee from the wrath to come?
Bear fruits worthy of repentance."

LUKE 3:7-8A

✠

John the Baptist is awesome. He faces everything without fear and holds strong to his purpose as he is true to himself. Instead of adjusting his message, John stands in the desert eating insects for protein and wearing a hairy coat to conjure truth through his fiery words. His passionate warnings come from his spiritual transformation—from a source of love rather than anger. A person must be bound by hope to work successfully with God.

His words in Luke hit hard: "You brood of vipers! Who warned you to flee from the wrath to come?" These aren't words found on Christmas cards. But John delivers his message with an earnest, direct plea to listeners to transform, to bear fruit worthy of repentance.

Jon Sobrino, a Jesuit priest from El Salvador, says that a "crucified people" is anyone who suffers systematic mistreatment but continues to maintain hope while continuously striving for justice and freedom and living joyfully. Sobrino teaches that authentic faith requires active participation, which drives believers to work within their environment. Faith is courage. Faith is action. The promises from God require complete trust within us despite clashing messages from the world.

John the Baptist lived in the wilderness, his very manner an example of the power of faith to transform lives. I wish to follow his example of faith—and that laid out by Fr. Sobrino. Christ's arrival requires active preparation instead of passive service. True faith means being joyful even in the chaos, loving fiercely, laughing often, speaking out in truth, and following these words with action.

As we celebrate Advent, let us move ahead in dance rather than merely holding on. And when we stumble, we keep going, bearing fruit and loving God and neighbor.

—Lester Mackenzie

PRAY

BROTHER JESUS, grant me the strength of John the Baptist—fearless in truth, fierce in love, and wise in the ways of the wilderness. Teach me when to speak, when to repent, and when to choose honey over locusts. *Amen.*

IV
Advent

Sunday

You have fed them with
the bread of tears;
you have given them bowls
of tears to drink.

Psalm 80:5

The feelings of grief are like laundry tumbling in a clothes dryer. The grays of loneliness, reds of anger, blacks of darkness, and minute greens of hope are all mingled and churning relentlessly inside. There is no timer on grief that dings when it is complete, beckoning you to open the door of your heart.

At dusk this evening, on this winter solstice, twelve of us gathered around our dining room table for a meal and a "Blue Christmas" liturgy. While the Advent season brings shimmering lights and joy, some sit in grief's long darkness from the loss of loved ones, health, jobs, dreams, or joy. God has fed them bread of tears and given them bowls of tears to drink.

Within minutes of sitting down, Nora, a recent widow, plunged us from our chit-chat about Christmas traditions to the depths of her loss, "During Larry's cancer, I felt helpless. It was like watching the sun slowly fade into darkness. I couldn't prop up the sun. All I could do was give him his medications, pray, and keep watch."

Nancy, fingering her necklace, shared, "I hear you. When my son was on life support, I felt powerless, angry at myself for handing him the car keys. And angry at God when he died." Fred spoke of his wife's drawn-out dementia, marking his change from being her carefree travel companion to her full-time caretaker. Things were getting glum. That was when empathy's light emerged from the darkness: nods of understanding, wet eyes, patting shoulders, and reassuring hands squeezing other's hands.

Then, an unexpected guest arrived: laughter. Tears of sorrow yielded to tears of hilarity as we shared one amusing, endearing story after another: "Manny was a crack-up; every Christmas, he would go outside our front door, ring the bell, and then serenade me with carols." Mark chuckled, "When Lisa was pregnant, she craved chocolate chip cookies and stomped around the house mimicking Cookie Monster, 'Me want cookies!'" Mary chimed in, "Nick's weakness was Payday candy bars. He would hide them in our bedpost. He never knew I knew!"

We didn't get around to praying the Blue Christmas liturgy. We didn't need to. For one evening, grief's churning within paused long enough for us to untangle the darkness wrapped around our hearts. Hiding in our recesses was the wonder of empathy, laughter, and hope. We were not alone. We shared one bread, one cup of sorrow, and great hope blended in full measure.

—Phil Beyer

PRAYER

KEEP WATCH, DEAR LORD, with those who work, or watch, or weep this night, and give thine angels charge over those who sleep. Tend the sick, Lord; give rest to the weary, bless the dying, soothe the suffering, pity the afflicted, shield the joyous; and all for thy love's sake. *Amen.*

—The Book of Common Prayer

Monday

But now, because you did not
believe my words, which will be
fulfilled in their time, you will become
mute, unable to speak, until the
day these things occur.

LUKE 1:20

When I was in seminary, I went on a three-day silent retreat with my classmates. I was in my middle year, and I could hardly stand it. I am not the type to stay silent! The experience certainly gave me a different insight into Zechariah.

Zechariah is naturally incredulous after being told that he and his wife, Elizabeth, will have a son. He and

Elizabeth are older and childless. So, when he hears Gabriel announcing the impending pregnancy, he naturally has a few questions—particularly wondering how God can possibly be right in saying that they will have a child. In response, Gabriel pronounces that Zechariah will have to endure a time of silence until John is born some nine months later.

Can you imagine what it must have been like for Elizabeth to be pregnant and have a mute husband? All the way through her pregnancy, her husband wouldn't have been able to offer any words of reassurance or love. He wouldn't have been able to tell her she looked beautiful or ask if she wanted a backrub. This period of silence must have been incredibly isolating for both Elizabeth and Zechariah.

One of the things I learned on my silent retreat is that there are many ways to communicate. At meals, we found ways to mime to one another if we needed salt or pepper, and during sessions, we found ways to glance at one another, connecting over something shared or thinking back to a different class. That experience makes me think of silence in a different way; maybe it even served to deepen the relationship between Zechariah and Elizabeth.

When you are forced to be silent, you start to notice things differently. You become more aware of the world around you; without the sound of your voice or thinking of what you will say next, you move into deeper listening. I wonder what Zechariah heard during the time he was silent. What did he see in his wife as she grew heavy with child? I wonder about the time Elizabeth and Mary spent together. What did Zechariah glean from their visit?

In a world so filled with noise, sometimes silence is the retreat we need—even, and especially when we don't want to undertake it.

—Jazzy Bostock

PRAY

GOD OF PEACE AND QUIET, help me to be still and know that you are God. Help me to hear the promises you have made me and believe them. Help me to be quiet and listen. *Amen.*

Tuesday

The angel said to her, "Do not be afraid, Mary, for you have found favor with God. And now, you will conceive in your womb and bear a son, and you will name him Jesus."

LUKE 1:30-31

Names are powerful.

The Bible is full of reminders of the importance of names: when someone's mission or character changes, often, so does their name: Abram becomes Abraham, Sarai becomes Sarah, and Jacob becomes Israel.

We pay a great deal of attention to what we name our children because we know that names carry identity; giving a child a name has a powerful influence on them for the rest of their lives.

The power of a name is treated so seriously in scripture that "taking a name"—using a name, invoking the name of God—has its own commandment. The third commandment prohibits using, invoking, or calling upon God's "name in vain." And when Jesus teaches us to pray, he begins by saying, "Our Father who is in heaven, hallowed (holy!) be God's name."

Ancient peoples knew that pronouncing or invoking a name doesn't just say something; it does something.

In linguistics, there is something called the "explicit performative utterance." An "explicit performative" is a sentence whose utterance, when said under appropriate conditions, brings about the state of affairs it signifies. In other words, saying the words accomplishes what the words say.

An example is when the chairperson of a meeting says, "The motion carries," or "The meeting is adjourned," or when an umpire says, "Play ball." A less happy example is when a supervisor says, "You're fired."

Under certain conditions, when certain people say certain words, the very action of saying the words accomplishes what the words say.

The very name of Jesus means "he will save," and Jesus's birth is the fulfillment of the prophecy of Emmanuel, a birth and a life that means "God is with us." To know Jesus's name is to know who Jesus is.

The name Jesus is an explicit performative utterance! Jesus's very name means and brings salvation.

To the degree we understand that we receive an early Christmas present: the knowledge that invoking the name of Jesus is an explicit performative utterance.

Under certain conditions—you're feeling helpless, unsure, slipping, falling, overwhelmed—saying certain words like "Jesus, please help me" accomplishes what the words say. Divine action is put into play. Things shift, sometimes outwardly, noticeably, rapidly, and sometimes inwardly, in our perspective or over time.

This happens when we call upon God's name. When we invoke God's name. When we draw upon the power of God's name.

—John Ohmer

PRAY

JESUS, we call upon your name here today. Remind us in these closing days of Advent and this Christmas season that it is you we seek. Let these holy days bring us closer to you. Jesus, do what you do best: save us from what besets us by filling us with your love. Fill us with your purpose. Enlighten and embolden our lives so that we might be light and encouragement to others. Help us to incarnate and live out your love in our daily lives, for you are Emmanuel, God with us. *Amen.*

Wednesday

When Elizabeth heard Mary's greeting,
the child leaped in her womb.
And Elizabeth was filled with the Holy
Spirit and exclaimed with a loud cry,
"Blessed are you among women, and
blessed is the fruit of your womb."

LUKE 1:41-42

Imagine the scene: Mary, a young woman, newly pregnant, rushes to see Elizabeth, her much older relative, who is also miraculously expecting. It's an unlikely meeting—two women whose lives have been upended by God's plans. And when Mary arrives, Elizabeth greets her with joy so overwhelming that her baby, the future John the Baptist, leaps in her womb. This moment could've been filled with uncertainty or fear, but instead, Mary responds with a song—the *Magnificat*.

Mary's song isn't just beautiful; it's bold. It's a proclamation of who God is and what God does. Mary starts by marveling at how God has chosen her, an ordinary girl from an ordinary town, for something extraordinary. "My soul magnifies the Lord, and my spirit rejoices in God my Savior" (verses 46-47). But Mary doesn't stop with personal praise; she zooms out to see the bigger picture of what God is doing for the world.

God's kingdom, she sings, flips everything upside down. The proud are scattered, the powerful are brought low, the humble are lifted, and the hungry are filled. This isn't a distant, theoretical hope—it's a reality breaking in with the coming of Jesus. Mary sees it and sings about it because she knows that God's promises aren't just words; they're active, alive, and coming to fruition through the child in her womb.

Advent is a season of waiting, but Mary's song reminds us that it's not a passive waiting. It's an active, hopeful anticipation. Mary sings as if the promises are already fulfilled because, in Jesus, they are. God's light is already shining, even if the world doesn't fully see it yet.

Mary could have responded with fear or doubt. She had plenty of reasons to—she was young, unmarried, and about to become the mother of the Messiah. But instead of letting fear take over, she trusted God and burst into a song of hope.

What about us? When life feels uncertain, do we sing like Mary? Do we trust God is at work, even when the path ahead is unclear? Advent invites us to echo Mary's song, to believe that God is turning the world upside down and bringing light into every corner of darkness.

Mary's faith is a reminder that God doesn't need the rich, the powerful, or the perfect to accomplish his purposes. He chooses ordinary people—like Mary, like you, like me—to carry God's light and hope into the world.

—Joseph Yoo

PRAY

LORD, give us a heart like Mary's, ready to trust and rejoice in your promises. Help us see your light breaking through in unexpected places, and let our lives sing of your love and faithfulness this Advent season. *Amen.*

Thursday

Restore us, O God of hosts;
show the light of your countenance,
and we shall be saved.

Psalm 80:7

✣

The rabbi moved her hands inward from the newly lit candles to her eyes and then explained the movement: "We draw the light of God back into ourselves as we celebrate Shabbat." Those gathered in celebration nodded at the beauty of the truth she had spoken. Some of us moved our hands to our eyes, calling the holiness of the moment into ourselves.

The Jewish tradition of gathering on Friday evening at sundown to mark the beginning of Shabbat is deeply beautiful and powerful. Shabbat candles are lit, and a blessing is recited to mark the beginning of a day of rest and spiritual focus.

We go and go and go so much in our lives; we create to-do lists and more to-do lists, and we don't mark off a time of rest and spiritual focus. We keep busy and stay busy.

And I wonder why.

We know the value of rest. We know the value of taking care of our selves and our souls. We know the value of sabbath. Yet we readily, almost pathologically, ignore it. We worship at the altar of the glorification of busy and invite endless chatter and movement to take up all the space in our selves. We go until we collapse on our sofas, falling asleep to whatever marginally interesting television show is playing, exhausted at the end of the day or week. We wake up tired, and we begin again.

The culture we live in this time of year is particularly dedicated to the celebration of more—more parties, more gifts, more decorations, more perfection in a quest for the "perfect" holiday. All these things, while fun (and I'm a fan of nothing exceeds like excess in the decoration department), consume our energy—our light. All of this activity keeps us from drawing the Light of God back into ourselves.

I wonder if we fear taking time to call the light of God back into ourselves. I wonder if we know, innately perhaps, that stopping to rest, to make time for spiritual focus, will change us. And while we may not like all of where we are, we do like what is known.

For better or worse, what is known is familiar, and we humans are creatures of the familiar.

The psalmist today says, "Restore us, O God of hosts; show the light of your countenance, and we shall be saved."

In this season of Advent, the church invites us to a time of restoration, reflection, and rest. Restore us, we pray. Remind us of the significance of drawing the light of God back into ourselves.

Creating regular time to draw the light of God into our selves and souls creates a way for the light to find its way into our corners and crevices, where we've hidden things about our selves and souls we don't want to face: the forgiveness we've denied, the anger we've justified grasping onto, the gifts of God we're refusing to use or misusing, the shame we've allowed to speak louder than God's love, the shame we transmit to others, the dreams we've abandoned, and the deep truths we don't want to hear.

Make no mistake, when I've gone on retreat, I've dropped into my muck and mud and found the Light of God amid all the primordial stuff I ignored or believed I had processed. I've stumbled over truths the Light illuminated, skinned my knees, and bruised myself in the fall, then discovered the beauty of the mess where I sat. It sounds lovely in hindsight, and it is, but it's often messy, hard work to draw the Light of God to one's interior and allow it to illuminate what we'd rather not see.

I wonder what might happen if we dedicated time each week, perhaps each day, to drawing the Light of God back into our selves, allowing God to show us the parts of our souls we are trying to ignore with our constant busyness, and reminding us to rest and refocus on God.

—*Laurie Brock*

PRAY

God of Light and Shadows, may we see your holiness in darkness and in light, drawing your wonder, your love, and your restoration into our weary and worried souls in the Name of your Son Jesus Christ. *Amen.*

Friday

Sing to the LORD a new song; sing to the LORD all the whole earth.

PSALM 96:1

Sigh. Like our Christmas tree's dry, sagging boughs, I feel wilted, just plain tired. Aunt Martha's once scrumptious sugar cookies are stale, and the leftovers in the fridge are well, leftover, and leftover again. My Christmas spirit is sputtering, running low on fumes. Is everything long awaited for now in my rear-view mirror? Groan.

My spirits brighten as I behold our manger scene under the tree, solitary, blanketed with fallen pine needles. Baby Jesus is in the manger. Mary and Joseph, shepherds, the lowing cattle, and angels are attending. The Magi are nearing, following their guiding light. In the stillness of this moment, gratitude seeps into my heart for the sacred wonder of Christ, the fulfillment of God's redemption. It dawns on me that the long-awaited one, Jesus, is before me, present in me, not in my rearview mirror. And that is worthy to be praised!

How shall I praise God? Deep within, my zany, spiritual wildness shouts, "Sing the song that is in your heart!" Hmm. Zechariah did that in Luke once God pressed the unmute button on him, singing, "By the tender mercy of our God, the dawn from on high will break upon us, to give light to those who sit in darkness and in the shadow of death, to guide our feet in into the way of peace."

Well, let me check what songs are on my heart's musical playlist. Ahh, at the top is Handel's *Messiah* and the "Hallelujah Chorus." I just gotta sing it a gazillion times, "For the Lord God omnipotent reigneth, Hallelujah! Hallelujah! Hallelujah! Hallelujah!"

Next on my list is Psalm 96 from today's readings, "Sing to the Lord a new song; sing to the Lord, all the earth. Sing to the Lord and bless his Name; proclaim the good news of his salvation from day to day..."

Take a listen to Psalm 148, "Hallelujah! Praise the Lord from the heavens; praise him the heights. Praise him, all you angels of his; praise him, all his host. Praise him, sun, and moon; praise him, all you shining stars…"

It is time to pause and reflect on the songs in your heart. Face it, there are a gazillion ways to praise Jesus, new each day. When we give ear to the songs of our hearts, we discover the one long-awaited—Jesus—is present in us. And that is what makes God's heart sing.

—*Phil Beyer*

PRAYER

JOY TO THE WORLD! the Lord is come: let earth receive her king; let every heart prepare him room, and heaven and nature sing, and heaven and nature sing and sing, and heaven, and heaven and nature sing. *Amen.*

—"Joy to the World," Isaac Watts

Saturday

She will bear a son, and you are to name him Jesus, for he will save his people from their sins.

Matthew 1:21

Joseph is told in a dream-like visitation that he and Mary are to name their son "Jesus." In this story, we learn that the very name of Jesus means "he will save" and that Jesus's birth is the fulfillment of the prophecy of Emmanuel, a birth and a life that means "God is with us."

To know Jesus's name is to know who Jesus is: Savior. To know Jesus's name is to know what Jesus does: he's one who saves.

But that begs the question: If Jesus is the Savior, what does it mean to save? The Greek word for save (*sozo*) can mean save in the sense of "keep from harm." It can mean "rescue." It can mean "heal." It can mean "liberate." You can be saved from drowning…you can be saved from sickness...you can be saved from slavery or bondage. You can be saved from sin or the power of evil.

As theologian William C. Placher put it in his book, *Jesus the Savior: The Meaning of Jesus Christ for Christian Faith*:

> We try to find fulfillment in things other than God, things like wealth, fame, success… [but none of it finally satisfies because they do not fill the God-shaped hole inside of us.] We are meant to be in relationship with God, but we have wandered off on the wrong path. We cannot figure out what shape our life should take. We carry around secret fears, we know how deep our hidden flaws are, how much more we could do to help others. We wonder what, if anything awaits us after we die. But Jesus is the savior. Jesus offers us hope that gets us past our failures and fears.

In the very name of Jesus, Emmanuel—God with us—we are reminded that God is not above us or indifferent to us and certainly not against us. God is not scolding or impatient or disappointed with us. Those are all human projections onto God.

God with us is God among us: God concerned, attentive, God for us, God understanding and patient and delighting in us. That's the God revealed in Jesus. Chances are that anyone who tells you otherwise has their own power issues and agenda because Jesus's very name means and brings *sozo*, salvation.

Do you get that? Have you received that early Christmas present yet? Christians rejoice at Christmastime not because we've had a good or successful year, not because of the gifts we give or receive, and not even because loved ones surround us.

No, Christians rejoice at Christmastime because Emmanuel: God is near. God has entered in. God is found not away from the doubts, uncertainties, and hustle and bustle of our days but in the midst of them.

—John Ohmer

PRAY

COME, THOU LONG-EXPECTED JESUS born to set thy people free; from our fears and sins release us, let us find our rest in thee. Israel's strength and consolation, hope of all the earth thou art: dear desire of every nation, joy of every longing heart. Born thy people to deliver, born a child, and yet a king, born to reign in us for ever, now thy gracious kingdom bring. *Amen.*

—"Come, Thou Long-Expected Jesus," Charles Wesley

Christmas

Christmas Day

How beautiful upon the mountains are the feet of the messenger who announces peace, who brings good news, who announces salvation, who says to Zion, "Your God reigns."

ISAIAH 52:7

If there is anything I think we can all agree on—regardless of age, sexuality, political affiliation, or anything else—it's that we all want peace. We pray for peace; we yearn for peace; we hope for a world with more peace and less war. And yet, in all of our praying and wishing and hoping and dreaming, what are we actually doing to create more peace? To bring more peace to earth?

This passage from Isaiah makes me think differently about the desire for peace. Instead of simply a destination, peace is a journey, a way to walk in the world. This makes peace less abstract and more direct. Peace is how we interact with the earth, others, and ourselves. Peace is how we travel, always learning and discerning, constantly adjusting and moving.

Peace is also something to be shared. If you are part of a worshiping community, you probably have a time in the service where you share the peace—which is often a favorite part. Sharing peace can be in a hug, a handshake, or the peace-sign fingers. It's a warm part of the service; sometimes, in my congregation, people use the peace time to catch up and chat.

In Isaiah and, indeed, at Christmastime, we are reminded that our responsibility isn't just to come and adore Jesus as our prince of peace but to take his message to heart. We are to walk in the way of peace and proclaim it to others. Peace is good news, salvation for those who hear it. This Christmas, take some time to cultivate peace in yourself and your home. So many things vie for our attention during this busy season but keep putting your hand on your heart, taking deep breaths, and coming back to God's peace.

—Jazzy Bostock

PRAY

ALMIGHTY GOD, kindle, we pray, in every heart the true love of peace, and guide with your wisdom those who take counsel for the nations of the earth, that in tranquility your dominion may increase until the earth is filled with the knowledge of your love; through Jesus Christ our Lord, who lives and reigns with you, in the unity of the Holy Spirit, one God, now and forever. *Amen.*

—The Book of Common Prayer

December 26
Feast of Saint Stephen

While they were stoning Stephen,
he prayed, "Lord Jesus, receive my
spirit." Then he knelt down
and cried out in a loud voice,
"Lord, do not hold this sin against
them." When he had said this, he died.

ACTS 7:59-60

Following the Christmas Day festivities, the church invites Christians to honor the first Christian martyr named Stephen. The transition seems forced because the church shifts from celebrating Christmas in Bethlehem to showing its dedication through persecution. But this is no accident. The nativity of Christ exceeds sentimental emotions because it summons believers to demonstrate fearless commitment while following gospel teachings.

Through his witness, Stephen demonstrated that he served Christ by dying for Christ. As a deacon in the church, Stephen was committed to service, caring for widows, and protecting the poor from neglect. Stephen understood that God uses faithful service to perform great deeds and that his humble tasks would result in divine blessings.

Stephen's life demonstrates how the church is more than merely a place of attendance because God has commissioned it to spread God's mission across the world. Gathering together allows us to receive the Good News, which transforms our hearts and compels us to share it with others. Attending worship services during Advent and Christmas is much more than observing a birth story since our true purpose is to become disciples, to respond to the life of Jesus, and to shine light in the darkness.

And there will be darkness. Opposition will arise. Proclaiming the bold love of Jesus exposes us to threats, and when we stand for justice, we often face resistance.

As Stephen faced his death, the heavens opened, and he saw the glory of God preparing to receive him. That is God's promise to us as well. God awaits to welcome us with loving arms.

Come to church. Hear the divine story afresh. Experience the light of Christ transforming your soul, and then go out into the world, speaking and living this love to all you meet.

—Lester Mackenzie

PRAY

EVERLIVING GOD, whose will it is that all should come to you through your Son Jesus Christ: Inspire our witness to him, that all may know the power of his forgiveness and the hope of his resurrection; who lives and reigns with you and the Holy Spirit, one God, now and for ever. *Amen.*

—The Book of Common Prayer

December 27
Feast of Saint John

This is the message we have heard
from him and proclaim to you,
that God is light and in him
there is no darkness at all.
If we say that we have fellowship with
him while we are walking in darkness,
we lie and do not do what is true;
but if we walk in the light
as he himself is in the light,
we have fellowship with one another.

1 John 1:5-7a

Light is a common metaphor for Jesus and Jesus's followers.

Jesus called himself "the light of the world." The author of 1 John says, "God is light and in him there is no darkness at all." And Jesus tells his disciples—then and now—that "you are the light of the world."

Think about the pronoun: you. You are the light of the world. You, yes, you. You are the light of the world. You are the light someone needs. You are helping someone overcome their darkness. You do this in your unique way when you let your light shine.

When Michael Jordan was inducted into the Hall of Fame for basketball, he told a story that became famous. During a game in which Jordan scored somewhere between 20 and 25 points in a row, one of the assistant coaches, Tex Winter, said to Jordan, "There's no 'I' in 'team.' Jordan said, "No, but there is an 'I' in 'win!'"

Jordan knew that if his t-e-a-m was going to w-i-n, he had to do what he was gifted at doing: score points. It's the same with you. You "walk in the light as [Jesus] himself is the light" when you use what you are good at. If you hide your light, you might as well be in the darkness. That's because the purpose of light, but especially your light, is to give light to others.

Lights are doing their job when they illuminate the area for the benefit of the people in the room. When the lights are doing their jobs, people don't walk around saying, "Wow, those are really good lights. What are they, tungsten-halogen incandescents or dimmable compact fluorescents, or do you suppose they are recessed T8's?"

In the Gospel of Matthew, Jesus says, "Let your light shine before others, so that they may see your good works and give glory to your Father in heaven." *So that* means the purpose, the reason, the goal of light. If the sentence stopped with "Let your light shine before others," then this might be a story about effective publicity, getting your fifteen minutes of light fame.

But Jesus says, "Let your light shine before others so that they may see your good works and give glory to your Father in heaven."

—John Ohmer

PRAY

GOD, you are the source of light and giver of our gifts. Give us the desire to always use our gifts to be light and good news to those closest to us, our community, and the wider world. *Amen.*

December 28
Feast of the Holy Innocents

Then was fulfilled what had been spoken through the prophet Jeremiah: "A voice was heard in Ramah, wailing and loud lamentation, Rachel weeping for her children; she refused to be consoled, because they are no more."

Matthew 2:17-18

Scene of the Massacre of the Innocents, painted by Léon Cogniet in 1824, shows a woman in the corner of two stone walls, one clearly in partial destruction. She clutches her child to her, her legs folded beneath her. Her hand partially covers her son's mouth, trying desperately to keep him from making any noise that may reveal them. The background figures are chaotic: women running with children under their arms, soldiers with swords, and small bodies cast on the ground. The painting is heartbreaking and upsetting.

When I look at the painting, I'm aware of her face. Cogniet paints her expression with powerful layers of terror, hope, dread, desperation, and exhaustion. She looks directly at us, seeemingly wondering if we are there to help her and her child. Will we offer her and her young son a place of refuge and care in the face of a cruel imperial decree, even when doing so may also put us in danger?

Are we part of the empire, soldiers, or citizens who care more about law and order than love and compassion? Are we there to expose her and her son so that mother and child will be separated from each other and the son surely slaughtered, and the mother left to grieve?

Now that we've seen her plight, we have a decision. Will we continue walking, ignoring the tragedy unfolding around us because it won't affect us, will it? Will we stop and wonder how we can help? Will we actually help?

Who are we, and what will we do? She wants to know.

Today is the Feast Day of the Holy Innocents, a day where we remember the infants who were mercilessly slaughtered by Herod's decree in his horrific display of power. This painting captures one heart-rending moment in that story. It captures the questions that mothers and fathers and parents with children who are still victims of heartless and callous political decrees and decisions ask us. They are looking at us from the ruins of war in Gaza, internment camps for undocumented immigrants, areas of our communities where the homes are unsafe, and places in our world devastated by global warming so that food no longer grows and children waste away.

What will we do when we see children suffering and dying? Who are we? Are we passersby, trying to avoid eye contact? Are we part of the system that justifies the slaughter of innocents for any number of reasons? Or are we willing to risk our own comfort and safety to respond in love and courage? In Cogniet's painting, the mother confronts us in our comfort and privilege. She wants to know if we will help her child, the child in our community, and the child across the globe.

What will we do? She is still asking us.

—Laurie Brock

PRAY

We remember today, O God, the slaughter of the holy innocents of Bethlehem by King Herod. Receive, we pray, into the arms of your mercy all innocent victims; and by your great might frustrate the designs of evil tyrants and establish your rule of justice, love, and peace; through Jesus Christ our Lord, who lives and reigns with you, in the unity of the Holy Spirit, one God, for ever and ever. *Amen.*

—The Book of Common Prayer

December 29

Nicodemus, who had gone to Jesus earlier, and who was one of them, asked, "Our law does not judge people without first giving them a hearing to find out what they are doing, does it?"

JOHN 7:50-51

✠

If the name Nicodemus sounds familiar to you, it should. He shows up earlier in John, in chapter 3, when Nicodemus comes to Jesus by night and has a confusing conversation about being born again. He leaves the encounter without making a clear commitment to Jesus. Nicodemus is often judged harshly for only coming to Jesus at night and for not having the courage to become a follower.

Today's passage from John is the second time we see Nicodemus. Now, he stands up for Jesus, using the law to ensure a fair hearing. We will see Nicodemus again after Jesus's crucifixion; in John 19, he provides the spices for Jesus's body and helps to prepare him for burial.

I love the arc of Nicodemus's faith story, and I love that we get to bear witness to it all. Often in the gospels, we have one-time encounters, and we're not really sure what happens to the one who was healed or the one who was saved. We see their immediate reaction but do not know how they are doing a few months—or even years—later.

Nicodemus has a slower faith conversion. He is hesitant at first to even come to Jesus, and even after their first conversation, Nicodemus remains unconvinced. He doesn't have a dramatic conversion so much as a slow change of heart. His story reminds me that God works with our willingness: all God needs is a small opening, and then, in time, the Spirit works with us on our unbelief.

Though Nicodemus isn't ready to follow Jesus during his life, he mourns him when he dies, showing up at the end in a profound way, a time when many of the other disciples have scattered with their grief and fear.

This story reminds me that our faith journeys are uniquely our own. We are not all supposed to be Peters—or James and John. Some of us might be more like Nicodemus, tentatively seeking out Christ for a one-time encounter that takes a while to grow in us. Whatever your spiritual journey, know that God loves you exactly as you are and exactly where you are, just as he loved Nicodemus.

—Jazzy Bostock

PRAY

ALMIGHTY GOD, come into my heart and plant a seed of faith. Nurture my curiosity and wonder. Help me to be honest about my unbelief. Lord, I trust that a willing heart is all you need to plant and nurture a seed that will grow into something more like faith. Help me to trust that you are with me on the journey. *Amen.*

December 30

O LORD my God, let this child's life
come into him again.

1 KINGS 17:21B

I had never received a hug from a furnace repairperson until today. Ronnie stepped into our kitchen from the garage, wiping his greasy hands with a rag, "All done, your heater's runnin' fine." His eyes widened, and he became still as he gazed at the cross, candle, and paper on the kitchen counter. After a while, I cleared my throat to break the overlong silence, "We keep a candle lit 24-7 by the cross and a prayer list to remind us to pray for others." Ronnie broke into a wide grin, threw his head back, and bellowed, "Let me tell ya a story."

Ronnie began, "My momma fell and had to be life-flighted to a hospital. She was in a coma for days, and no one could tell us what was wrong. I was mad and stomped around the lobby, just fuming. A stranger walked up to me, said he was a preacher, and asked to pray with me. I don't much pray, but I let him go ahead, right there in the lobby. Darndest thing. The next morning in the cafeteria, the preacher came up to my wife and me and said, 'God's got this.' Two hours later, the doctors told us Momma would live. Now, she's back home, going to church, and driving to the grocery store."

Shifting his feet, Ronnie watched the candle flicker. "After Momma's recovery, I started going to church. Strange, but good stuff keeps happenin' to me. One Sunday, I was just sitting there in church and felt lifted up and peaceful. After the service, a bunch of folks came up and hugged me. Weird things like that, you know. And now I see your candle here, and you all praying for people..." At that, right there in the kitchen, Ronnie hugged me. "Thanks for listening to my story."

As I was writing a check, Ronnie was busy adding names to our prayer list. We hugged again, slapping backs, and I vowed to pray for him and those on the list.

After Ronnie left, I reflected on how God is present in healing, which often leads to faith. We have a God who makes weird but good things happen. God was at work in Ronnie's life experience just as God was at work with Elijah and Jesus in today's scripture, inspiring the miraculous healing of children and a widow and temple official coming to faith. And God was present in a preacher in a hospital lobby, folks hugging in a church, and a repairperson standing in a kitchen gazing at a candle and sharing his budding faith journey.

—Phil Beyer

PRAYER

AND I HEARD A LOUD VOICE from the throne saying, "See, the home of God is among mortals. He will dwell with them; they will be his peoples, and God himself will be with them."

—Revelation 21:3

December 31

I am the light of the world.
Whoever follows me
will never walk in darkness
but will have the light of life.

JOHN 8:12

✠

A door stands before you. Have you observed this door before and chosen not to enter it? Have you purposefully remained unconscious of it?

Jesus illuminates this door in his divine way by staying next to it while gently guiding you toward the light of transformation.

New beginnings can be frightening. Sometimes, discomfort seems safer than exploring unfamiliar places. Maybe you've had the experience of someone recognizing something in you that you weren't ready to explore. That's what happened with me.

My bishop at the time, Jon Bruno, saw something in me that I didn't see at first. He kept encouraging me to explore unfamiliar paths. During my early unfolding in ministry, Bishop Chet Talton made room for me to find my voice. These leaders and others expressed Christ's invitation to discipleship by extending invitations to others to move deeper into the faith. South African activist Steve Biko once said, "The most potent weapon in the hands of the oppressor is the mind of the oppressed." Freedom starts from within as individuals accept an invitation to new perspectives about their capabilities and what they can achieve.

The light of Jesus illuminates both the current state and future possibilities in life. Through his wisdom, Jesus shatters the false narratives that proclaim I am not enough, that I am held captive by my previous self. The paths I avoided before now shine under his light as promising new possibilities.

The door to the Light stands wide open, and I must take the necessary step to pass through it. Jesus is waiting to transform me through his love.

—*Lester Mackenzie*

PRAY

Jesus, please open my spiritual eyes to see the Light and hear the invitation and know that my heart deserves fresh beginnings. Help me to respond to the Light's summons by stepping toward it. *Amen.*

January 1
Feast of the Holy Name

When the angels had left them and gone into heaven, the shepherds said to one another, "Let us go now to Bethlehem and see this thing that has taken place, which the Lord has made known to us." So they went with haste and found Mary and Joseph, and the child lying in the manger. When they saw this, they made known what had been told them about this child; and all who heard it were amazed at what the shepherds told them.

LUKE 2:15-18

The shepherds were the first to hear the good news of Jesus's birth. Think about that for a second. Not kings, not priests, not the elite, but shepherds—ordinary people working the night shift, probably smelling a bit like their sheep. When the angel appeared, they were terrified (who wouldn't be?), but the message they received was nothing short of incredible: "To you is born this day in the city of David a Savior, who is the Messiah, the Lord" (Luke 2:11).

What did they do? They didn't sit around debating theology or overthinking the message; they didn't create a committee to oversee subcommittees to respond to the angel's message. They said, "Let's go!" and hurried off to Bethlehem to see for themselves. That's the kind of Advent faith we're invited into—a faith that hears the good news and moves, a faith that doesn't wait for every question to be answered but responds with wonder and curiosity.

When the shepherds found Mary, Joseph, and the baby lying in the manger, they couldn't keep the news to themselves. They told everyone what they had seen, and people were amazed. These were ordinary folks witnessing an extraordinary moment, and they let their excitement spill over. I wonder: When was the last time we were so moved by the good news of Jesus that we couldn't help but share it? Have we heard the story so many times that we've forgotten how truly incredible it is?

Then there's Mary. While the shepherds are out telling everyone, Mary treasures all these things and ponders them in her heart. Can you imagine what she was feeling? She had just given birth (to the Son of God, no less). She's exhausted and overwhelmed yet deeply aware that this moment is holy. Advent invites us to do what Mary did—to pause, reflect, and treasure in our hearts what God is doing in our lives.

But Advent also invites us to be like the shepherds, who left the manger glorifying and praising God. They didn't stay in the glow of the manger forever; they returned to their fields, but they returned forever changed. The good news of Jesus didn't just stay in Bethlehem—it went with them into their ordinary lives.

This Advent, we're reminded that the story of Jesus is for everyone: the tired, the messy, the ordinary. It's for shepherds and kings, for the broken and the hopeful. It's for you. And just like the shepherds, we're invited to share it. The light of Christ has come into the world, and it's too good to keep to ourselves.

—Joseph Yoo

PRAY

LORD, give me the wonder of the shepherds and the quiet trust of Mary. Help me to treasure the gift of Jesus and share his light with the world. May your love and joy overflow in my heart this Advent season and beyond. *Amen.*

January 2

Suddenly an angel touched him and said to him, "Get up and eat." He looked, and there at his head was a cake baked on hot stones, and a jar of water. He ate and drank, and lay down again.

1 Kings 19:5b-6

This is a hard story. Elijah runs away after an epic battle, feeling like he wants to give up. He lies down under a broom bush with the intent of letting himself perish. But God has other plans. God wants to see each of us thriving and living. To that end, God sends an angel to care for Elijah, to offer him a jar of water and something to eat. In some translations, Elijah is offered bread; in others, a hot cake. I like the translation of cake—because of personal preference—but either way, this is such a tangible act of care and concern that it moves me.

Sometimes we reference God as our Father, which is a metaphor with limitations. One of its limitations is that we equate this fatherliness in God to a kind of disciplinary parental figure, someone there to keep us in line and make sure we are doing what we ought to. The story we read today of God caring for Elijah shows such a motherly love, caring for her child enough to get him a snack and a drink of water and let him rest.

Many times in my life, the biggest problems I have in a day could be cured, or at least put into perspective, with the same formula: a snack, a drink of water, a nap, and an expression of love. And yet, we resist God caring for us in this way, thinking somehow that it is more faithful to push through, to grin and bear it, to endure and suffer along the way.

In caring for Elijah with this tenderness, God cares for us, too. God shows us that it is okay to rest, especially when we have been through something grueling. God sends helpers like angels to remind us to hydrate and sleep; sometimes, the angels might be dropping off a meal.

Maybe you are feeling like Elijah, in need of this care. Or perhaps this week, you have something extra to give, and you can be someone's angel, offering them the sustenance they need to keep going.

—*Jazzy Bostock*

PRAY

CARING SPIRIT, descend on me and enter into my life today. Help me to care for myself with the basics: bread, water, and rest. If that's all I can do, Lord, bless it to your service. If I have the capacity to share with someone else, show me who to share with. Direct me toward someone in need of a piece of grace, and help me to give it. All this I pray in the beautiful name of Jesus. *Amen.*

January 3

I am the good shepherd.
I know my own and my own know me,
just as the Father knows me
and I know the Father.
And I lay down my life for the sheep.

JOHN 10:14-15

The image of Jesus as a good shepherd is an ancient one. Throughout the Old Testament, God is often thought of as a shepherd, and everyone from Moses to Isaiah to Zachariah refers to God as a shepherd, perhaps most famously in Psalm 23: "The Lord is my shepherd, I shall not be in want, He makes me lie down in green pastures and leads me beside still waters."

Seeing Jesus as a good shepherd can be a powerful metaphor and affect how you make decisions because of the relationship between shepherds and sheep. Depending on the type of shepherd and the terrain, shepherds may lead their sheep from the front, behind, or—with help—from the left and right sides of the flock.

Shepherds sometimes lead from the front. They walk slowly, scoping out the terrain, looking for greener pastures. The sheep follow them, or more accurately, follow their voice. This is an image of God as inspiration, someone you look up to, and someone whose guidance you seek.

Shepherds also sometimes lead from behind. They follow the flock because from behind, you can see where the flock is going and keep it in sight. They scan the flock, watching for overall direction and keeping their eyes out for danger. This is an image of God as protector: God as someone quite literally behind you, as in "I've got your back."

And sometimes shepherds, with help, lead from beside. Shepherds, after all, use sheepdogs. And it is sheepdogs who actually do the herding; sheepdogs keep the flock together by nipping at the heels of sheep who are going astray.

Do you see how having an image of the Lord as your shepherd affects your decisions?

God is someone in front of you, inspiring you, someone you can look up to, someone to guide you, someone who inspires us.

God is also someone behind you, backing you, believing in you, urging you on, encouraging you, not always guiding you every step of the way, but watching your overall direction. God is someone who gives us confidence.

And God is sometimes sending out "sheepdogs" to keep you from going too far astray. Like a good shepherd, God sometimes uses helpers, people (or sometimes life events) who serve to "nip us in the heels" and get us back in line when we are drifting too far into dangerous territory. God is someone who protects us.

Having an image of the Lord as your shepherd affects the way you make decisions because you have a source of inspiration, confidence, and protection—before you, behind you, and all around.

—John Ohmer

PRAY

O God, whose Son Jesus is the good shepherd of your people: Grant that when we hear his voice we may know him who calls us each by name, and follow where he leads; who, with you and the Holy Spirit, lives and reigns, one God, for ever and ever. *Amen.*

—The Book of Common Prayer

January 4

The words that I say to you
I do not speak on my own;
but the Father who dwells in me
does his works. Believe me that
I am in the Father and
the Father is in me.

John 14:10b-11a

✥

Chicago's harsh winters rarely kept Gram from walking six blocks to Mass each morning dressed in the same dark blue dress with white polka dots and threadbare babushka covering her head. She was widowed at an early age, and when my parents married, Gram resided with them and eventually cared for my older sister, brother, and me.

To me, Gram was God with skin on. As I toddled near her easy chair, she swept me onto her lap and crisscrossed her plump arms around my chest. Nuzzling my ear, Gram whispered, "You are the apple of my eye." Wrapped in the coverlet of her arms, listening to her heartbeat, I felt one with her, loved and cherished, for I was the apple of her eye.

Years later, after Gram's death, my siblings and I were recounting "Gram stories." I jested, "Gram loved me the most! I was the apple of her eye!" My siblings took exception, asserting Gram had reassured each of them that they were the apple of her eye. We laughed, allowing the tender message to sink in: Gram had intimately loved us, a love that forever dwells in us.

We don't know much about Jesus's formative years, but I can almost see Mary holding Jesus tight, humming, the vibrations soothing her beloved, divine child. Or I muse that years later, as Jesus toddled by, Joseph put down the mallet and chisel of his trade to gather up Jesus in his arms to bless him. It strikes me that Jesus radiated love because he was humanly and divinely loved.

In today's gospel, Jesus reveals his intimate oneness with God the Father, "Believe me that I am in the Father and the Father is in me…." Seated amongst the disciples, Jesus is God with skin on, visible, touchable, and relatable. To touch Jesus is to touch God. Jesus incarnate abides in the world, emulating the works of the Father, living the life God intends for all humanity.

Now, in my twilight years, I still totter through life, committing goofy missteps, miscues, and faux pas. Through life's travails and joys, I have learned to trust the tangible human and divine presence that abides in me. I am loved. Therefore, I love, seeking to joyfully live the way, the truth, and the life God intended.

—*Phil Beyer*

PRAY

The Christ-child lay on Mary's lap, His hair was like a light. (O weary, weary, were the world, But here is all aright.) The Christ-child lay on Mary's heart, His hair was like a fire. (O weary, weary is the world, But here the world's desire.)

—"The Christ-child Lay on Mary's Lap"

January 5

Jesus said to them,
"Unbind him, and let him go."

JOHN 11:44B

We have just concluded Advent, a season of waiting, but let's be honest—many of us don't wait well. I know I don't. We get impatient if the line at the coffee shop takes longer than we'd want. I'm known to say, "No Wi-Fi is better than slow Wi-Fi," because when Wi-Fi lags, it's the worst (first-world problems, eh?).

Imagine waiting not minutes, not hours, but for four long days. That's what Mary and Martha endure after Lazarus, their brother, dies. Four days of wondering, "Where is Jesus?" Four days of silence. Four days of heartbreak. When

Jesus finally shows up, Martha can't help but say what we've all felt at some point: "Lord, if you had been here, my brother would not have died."

Can you hear the pain in her words? The unspoken questions? "Why did you take so long? Don't you care?" Martha's honesty is quite refreshing. She doesn't attempt to hide her disappointment, and yet—here's the beautiful part—she still believes. "But even now," she confesses, "I know that God will give you whatever you ask of him."

That's a picture of faith in the waiting: a trust that holds on, even when life doesn't make sense.

Jesus responds with the words all of us Christians are familiar with: "I am the resurrection and the life. Those who believe in me, even though they die, will live." And then, Jesus asks Martha a personal (yet universal) question: "Do you believe this?"

Our journey through Advent and Christmas asks us the same question. Do we believe that Jesus is the resurrection and the life? Do we trust that he brings light into our darkness and offers hope in our despair?

It's easy to say "yes" when life is good and everything is going according to plan. But how often does life go according to our set plans? What about when you're stuck in a season of waiting, carrying the weight of uncertainty, unanswered prayers, and broken dreams?

Martha's response gives us hope: "Yes, Lord, I believe."

Then Jesus does the wildly unexpected. He goes to Lazarus's tomb, prays, and calls his friend to come out of the grave. And Lazarus does! Death doesn't get the final word. Jesus does.

May this story remind us that the life of faith isn't just about looking back at Jesus's birth or looking forward to his return. It's about trusting that he is the resurrection and life right now, in seasons of blessings and abundance, but also in seasons of waiting, even in places that feel like tombs.

Jesus is present, calling us—inviting us—to step into the light of God's love.

So, where do you need resurrection? Maybe it's a relationship, a hope you've buried, or a part of your faith that feels lifeless. The good news is that Jesus is still calling. Still shining light into darkness. Still asking, "Do you believe this?"

—Joseph Yoo

PRAY

LORD, teach me to trust you even in the waiting. Bring your resurrection power into the places where I feel stuck or broken. Help me to hear your voice calling me into the light of your love. I believe, Lord—help my unbelief. *Amen.*

January 6
Epiphany

When they had heard the king,
they set out; and there, ahead of them,
went the star that they had seen
at its rising, until it stopped over the place
where the child was.
When they saw that the star had stopped,
they were overwhelmed with joy.

MATTHEW 2:9-10

Of all the ways to get from one place to another—maps, GPS, even the directions so often used by my grandmother that included things like, "Turn at the tree that used to be in front of the old Jones house…you know, the one that the tornado destroyed about 25 years ago"—I can think of nothing as inefficient as a star.

And yet humans have navigated by stars for centuries. Celestial navigation, using stars and planets to determine where on Earth you were, was the common way sailors navigated until the late twentieth century. Using the North Star and other navigational stars, the place of the constellations in the sky (which change location depending on the time of year), and far more intricate knowledge than I could attempt to explain, travelers could know where they were and what direction in which they needed to go.

One necessary part for celestial navigation by stars is darkness, something we modern humans in many parts of the world seem less and less able to find. Our desire to lighten the darkness with streetlights and security lights and motion sensor lights and decorative lights have created a world that is overwhelmed with light. As we add more and more artificial light to lighten our darkness, we pollute our night skies. We become less able to see the magnificent, mysterious night skies.

The Milky Way, one of the most stunning celestial displays to entrance, guide, and captivate humans for eons, is now not visible by 99 percent of people living in the United

States and a third of the people living in the world because of all of our artificial light. Our desire to lighten our lives and eradicate darkness has left us unable to see the guiding stars, which are only visible in the holiness of darkness.

With all our language around light in Christianity, we may miss that darkness is also essential for the fullness of our faith. Humans encounter God in the dark of night, from angels startling shepherds to Mary Magdalene encountering the Risen Christ in the darkness of morning. We need darkness to see God. The Magi follow a star that we can guess is visible at its brightest at night. They move in the darkness to follow the star to the Christ Child. We need the darkness to illumine some holy ways that cannot be seen in the light of day.

We have too often associated darkness with things to be avoided, things that are bad. The Magi remind us that darkness is necessary for us to see the light, to be guided not only by light but with the light in partnership with the darkness. In darkness, we see less with our eyes and more with our souls. This Epiphany, turn off the lights. Light a candle. Sit in the holy darkness and let God lead you home by another path.

—Laurie Brock

PRAY

O God, by the leading of a star you manifested your only Son to the peoples of the earth: Lead us, who know you now by faith, to your presence, where we may see your glory face to face; through Jesus Christ our Lord, who lives and reigns with you and the Holy Spirit, one God, now and for ever. *Amen.*

—The Book of Common Prayer

About the Authors

Phil Beyer has a passion for serving the unhoused, incarcerated, and addicted and missions in Haiti. He is a retired businessperson, author, and avid gardener who lives in Tallahassee, Florida, with Jeanie, his wife of 53 years and a retired archdeacon of the Diocese of Florida. They have two adult children and two grandchildren. Jeanie and Phil worship at St. John's Episcopal Church in Tallahassee.

Jazzy Bostock, a kanaka maoli, Episcopal priest, farmer, wife, and mom, lives and works in Waianae, Hawaii.

Laurie Brock has served as rector of St. Michael the Archangel in Lexington, Kentucky, since 2010. She's the author of several books, including *Where God Hides Holiness, Horses Speak of God: How Horses Can Teach Us to Listen and Be Transformed, God, Grace, and Horses*, and her latest one, *Souvenirs of the Holy.* She is a frequent contributor to books and online spirituality resources and a speaker at local and national events about faith.

Lester V. Mackenzie is a South African–born, third-generation priest who now serves as Chief of Mission Program for the Presiding Bishop of The Episcopal Church. A dynamic speaker, executive coach, and musician, he weaves Ubuntu, rhythm, and deep prayer into every encounter, turning each heartbeat into a cadence of reconciliation and hope.

John Ohmer recently retired from thirty years of full-time ministry in the Episcopal Church and currently serves part-time as coordinator of the Lay Preacher Program for the Episcopal Preaching Foundation. In his ministry, he has served as the Upper School Chaplain at St. Christopher's School in Richmond, Virginia; Interim Dean for the Cathedral of All Souls in Asheville, NC, and Rector of the Falls Church Episcopal in Falls Church, Virginia, among other calls. Before ordination, he had a brief career in government, working as a Capitol Hill and presidential campaign staff member, and as a press secretary and speech writer in his home state of Indiana. His wife, Mary, is a public school teacher; they have three grown-and-flown children and recently welcomed their first grandchild. They spend their free time reading, hiking, and figuring out how to tire out their tireless Border Collie-Springer Spaniel mix named Sadie.

Joseph Yoo is the vicar of Mosaic Episcopal Church, a church plant in the Diocese of Texas. He is also the author of *When the Saints Go Flying In*. He and his wife, Rahel, have a son, Nathanael.

About Forward Movement

Forward Movement inspires disciples and empowers evangelists. We live out our call as a discipleship ministry by publishing daily reflections and online resources. People around the world read daily devotions through *Forward Day by Day*, which is also available in Spanish (*Adelante Día a Día*) and Braille, online, as a podcast, and as an app for your smartphone.

A ministry of the Episcopal Church since 1935, Forward Movement is a nonprofit organization funded by sales of resources and gifts from generous donors.

Learn more about Forward Movement and our work at forwardmovement.org or venadelante.org.